ROCK 'N' ROLL WITCH

WITCH

*A Memoir of Sex Magick,
Drugs, & Rock 'N' Roll*

By

Pleasant Gehman

PUNK HOSTAGE PRESS

ROCK 'N' ROLL WITCH

A Memoir of Sex Magick, Drugs & Rock 'N' Roll

Illustrations
Pleasant Gehman

Introduction
Pamela Des Barres

Foreword
Theresa Kereakes

Cover Layout
Natasha Vetlugin

Author Photo
Christina L. Hughes

Punk Hostage Press
Hollywood, USA
www.punkhostagepress.com

ROCK'N'ROLL WITCH

BY PLEASANT GEHMAN

*PUNK*HOSTAGE*PRESS*

To my brother Chuckles aka Steffenson

I will love you forever

Charles R. Gehman 2/13/61 – 8/6/20

TABLE OF CONTENTS

INTRODUCTION

Pleasant's most peaceful place as a little girl was atop a cool marble slab at her local cemetery, where she began writing about her life a great blessing for you, dear reader. Our curious little doll became a preeminent Punkromancer, cavorting with the dangerous elite at her Hollywood hangout, Disgraceland. She published one of the first fanzines, *Lobotomy: the Brainless Magazine*, featuring the entire burgeoning LA punk scene between its covers, and fronted The Screaming Sirens, a vividly entrancing all-femme band... not to mention romping with the likes of Iggy Pop. As Princess Farhana, Pleasant has taken her belly dancing and simmering burlesque exploits to packed audiences worldwide. She listens to her prescient inner "Voice," which continues to lead her into all manner of scintillating adventures. Trust me when I say that these pages, full of eloquence and outrage, can barely contain Pleasant Gehman's effusive ebullience.

-Pamela Des Barres

FOREWORD

The weird and whimsical tales told by Hollywood have always seemed to match the *normal* life for our subculture at the intersection of punk rock and the supernatural. In this memoir, Pleasant Gehman tells her own whimsical, weird stories, but they're all true. This is a collection of experiences from her enchanted life.

Metaphysics have informed art and science since the beginning of time. Otherworldly characters fascinate us; some of our favorite rock songs are about Welsh witches, magic, and the ghosts of dead lovers. Creatures divine and dreadful populate literature and cinema from the Sirens in *Homer's Odyssey* to the Three Witches in Shakespeare's *MacBeth,* Mary Shelley's *Frankenstein* and all the monsters dead and undead that followed, including Anne Rice's sexy vampires. The success of films like *Ghost, The Craft, The Addams Family* and *Practical Magic,* not to mention *Harry Potter* put the supernatural into the mainstream. The expansive genre of metaphysical, gothic, witch/warlock/magician stories prove people want to be in touch with the other, unexplained side.

In the 1950s, rock'n'roll was denounced as "The Devil's Music", which not coincidentally, is also the name of Pleasant's podcast. In the early twentieth century, blues icon Robert Johnson was rumored to have sold his soul to The Devil. His *Crossroads Blues* led directly to Led Zeppelin's embrace of the dark magus, Aleister Crowley... and for those of us who know, all this is also *normal*.

Cemeteries have thus always been a punk rock amusement park. One of my fondest memories of an Easter Sunday tramp to commune with the spirit of Douglas Fairbanks gone almost deadly wrong is recalled in these pages. Pleasant's stories define the aphorism "truth is stranger than fiction" and she fills them with such vivid detail that you aren't reading the story, you're *in* the story. Her forthright evaluations are straight-up diary entry/secret thoughts; her scrapes with danger are transformative; they unlock mysteries. And what is art but the translation of mystery into understanding? Get in-the-know and take delight in what Pleasant reveals.

-Theresa Kereakes

"The world is full of magic things
patiently waiting for our senses to grow sharper."

-William Butler Yeats

LITTLE LAMB

Remember me as you pass by
As you are now so once was I
As I am now so you will be
Prepare for death and follow me

Indian Hill Cemetery sits high upon a summit overlooking the Connecticut River. Built on what had once been Wangunk land, the history is a bit different from the other historical graveyards that piggybacked on the burial grounds of indigenous people. Apparently, the hilltop site, the highest in the Middletown area, had once functioned as a lookout to watch for early settlers and enemy tribes. Dedicated in 1850 at the height of the Victorian period, Indian Hill is both a city of the dead and a paean to the excessive architectural grandeur of the time; it is also a beautiful example of the verdant, park-like beauty inspired by the Rural Cemetery Movement from that era.

The tranquil grounds are everything Edgar Allen Poe ever dreamed of and more, forty acres of a necromancer's wet dream. Towering over the ancient shade trees, Russell Chapel is a Gothic Revival masterpiece of Portland brownstone with a gigantic cast bronze bell mounted in the tower. When it tolls, the eerie sound carries over the grounds, causing flocks of nesting crows to scatter. Opulent Greek Revival mausoleums were built into the hillside, many overgrown with decades worth of ivy. Tall obelisks capped with carved mourning drapes stand watch over the resting places of whaling ship captains and wealthy local merchants. Sandstone reflection benches had been carefully sculpted to appear as though they were made of wooden logs; weeping marble angels kneel over raised tombs. Ancient slate headstones with winged Death's Heads bear the macabre rhyming verses commonly used as epitaphs in New England.

** ** **

I grew up as a latchkey kid in Middletown, Connecticut during the 1960s. It had once been a bustling whaling and Caribbean trade port, but at the time, it was a semi-rural, sleepy New England town surrounded by meadows, forests, and Butternut Hollow, where clear icy spring water bubbled up directly from the ground. My siblings and I walked to and from Stillman School on Loveland Street unaccompanied every day, as did all the other children; back then, it was normal. However, my own childhood was *anything* but.

My newly divorced mom was the premiere subject of gossip on our street. Middletown residents were mostly Sicilian or Polish Catholics, and single mothers were so unusual in those days that the mere sight of her raised eyebrows. She worked in the Theater Department at Wesleyan University, and the divide between Townies and Academics had been in place for decades. During The Summer Of Love, the gap widened. By 1968, my mother regularly held open houses frequented by her theater students, and the neighbor's fascination with our family had turned to astonishment. Our home was frequented by bearded hippies students swathed in love beads and tie-dye, each with their Townie teenybopper girlfriend in tow. Modern dance majors from New York City, flagrantly braless under their Danskin leotards, wandered in carrying as many bottles of Mateus wine as they could hold. Our babysitters, a hulking trio of Dashiki, clad football players from the

Wesleyan Cardinals, were regulars: the word on campus was that they'd started their own local Black Panther chapter.

Those gatherings were always fun and stimulating to my siblings and me, with acting scenes rehearsed in the living room while everyone else crowded around the kitchen table discussing plans to attend the Vietnam War Moratorium in Washington, DC. But even better, us kids had the run of the entire campus. Free range wasn't the word for us; we were *feral*. None of the buildings were ever locked, so my brother Charlie and I played Hide And Seek in the corridors of the dormitories or crashed afternoon beer bashes at frat houses. We'd hang out in Theater '92 watching set construction or luxurious period costumes getting embellished with lace and faux pearls. We were the audience during tech rehearsals for Shakespearian plays, African dance and drumming, or the musical comedies my mom directed, like the current Broadway hit *Celebration* or Cole Porter's classic *Anything Goes*. Charlie and I always slipped into the Film Department's amphitheater classroom at night because it was next door to our house. We'd lay on our stomachs under the desks watching age inappropriate films like Luis Bunuel and Salvador Dali's surrealist *Un Chien Andalou* or Todd Browning's carnival masterpiece *Freaks*. After school, we'd sneak into the Science Department to ogle the ancient specimens preserved in thick 1930s glass jars filled with formaldehyde or to the lift the tarps to look at the cadavers being dissected by Medical School students.

All of this was an interesting if unconventional way to grow up, but Middletown itself had an odd, much darker side, too. In addition to Indian Hill Cemetery, it was also home to Connecticut Valley Hospital, an imposing group of brick buildings built in 1868 that had once been known as Connecticut Hospital For The Insane. My family lived on Warren Street, directly across from what is now Wesleyan's Snyder Ice Rink. When I was little, it was a huge vacant lot surrounding a junkyard full of the mangled hulks of vintage automobiles, old mattresses with the springs hanging out, discarded toilets and rust-eaten earth moving equipment. Behind it, a group of hoodlum greasers had squatted out a dilapidated shed, using it as their secret illegal hot rod club. Charlie and I spied on them as they worked on their rides at twilight. Lucky Strikes hanging from the side of their lips, they'd cuss incessantly, brandishing wrenches at each other while tweaking ancient engines. Their girlfriends were all slutty-looking teenagers cracking their gum while chain smoking. They rocked big bouffant hairdo's and were poured into tight pastel sleeveless tops with black bra straps hanging out and sleek, front-seamed black stretch pants. They'd gossip in whispers as they looked on at the guys from dilapidated lawn chairs. Everybody guzzled beer non-stop, winging the empties as far as they could into the trash heap, guffawing each time the glass bottles exploded.

At the end of my street was Long Lane School For Girls, also built in 1868, which was the Connecticut state reformatory. A high-security prison for juveniles, everyone in town assumed the worst about the conditions there. It was widely rumored that the inmates were shackled to the beds. They all wore uniforms with stockings signifying their status: white stockings meant the girls were well-behaved and low-risk so they had privileges; black stockings were classified as Dangerous Inmates. Sometimes, on Main Street, I'd see the White Stocking Girls on their once-a-week afternoon leave. Without realizing they were adolescent foster kids just a handful of years older than me, I breathed in every iota of what I saw as their criminal glamour.

A few times each month, Warren Street turned chaotic when one of the Black Stockings made an escape attempt. Our whole neighborhood could hear the emergency alarms screaming from across the fields. Nosy Mrs. Hunt, the neighbor who was most scandalized by my mom's divorcee status, would always pop her head out her front door for a view of the action. Charlie and I, plus all the kids we played with, hopped on our bikes with everyone's unleashed dogs bounding alongside, heading towards Long Lane's cow pastures. Naturally, we were hoping to catch a glimpse of the action and maybe even hide one of the girls in our garage, but the cops always chased us away.

As exciting as this was, my absolute favorite place was Indian Hill Cemetery. The ornately decorated heavy wrought iron gates were directly across the street from the Wesleyan campus and a just a few blocks down Vine Street from my house. Every day after school, rain or shine I'd pedal furiously towards the graveyard on the pinstriped teal metal flake Schwinn bike I'd gotten for my tenth birthday. Indian Hill was like a magnet to me; it was an *addiction.* I couldn't stay away. Often, I'd go with Charlie or my best friend Joan Stern, but mostly I went alone. I'd spend entire days there in the muggy New England summers, lying on top of cool marble tombs writing in my diary while listening to birds chirping in the giant fir trees. It was so peaceful and serene that you could hear bumble bees buzzing around the newly placed Gladiola bouquets on the nearby graves. Sometimes I'd just ride my bike around the long concentric paths exploring all the different sections.

> *A silent thought a secret tear*
> *Keeps your memory ever dear*

It was on one of these jaunts that I came upon a subdivision I'd somehow never noticed before. Many of the graves dated from the time the memorial park had first opened; the fancy script epitaphs were almost indecipherable. I recall unmown grass interspersed with dirt patches and wondered if this was because there were no living family members left to care for their dead. The entire area seemed different than the rest of the cemetery; it was off the beaten path, or at least the ones I'd usually take, no wonder I'd overlooked it. Dismounting my bike, I saw graves dating from the Civil War through World War I that were obviously for veterans; short cast iron poles devoid of their flags were sunk into the ground next to each plot. A few Edwardian era slate and sandstone *stelae* tilted at strange angles in the uneven ground. The most current headstones appeared to date from the time of the Spanish Flu; 1918 through the early 1920s.

Just beyond the soldiers, I spotted a cluster of what appeared to be miniature gravestones nestled into in a wildflower meadow. The area was overgrown with tall grass, blooming gaily with Bachelor's Buttons, Dandelions and Black-eyed Susans. Always a bookworm, I'd heard of Potter's Fields and wondered if that's what *this* was. Wading through the crabgrass, I got to the first headstone, which seen up close, made me realize it actually *was* considerably smaller than the standard size. It was so eroded it looked like a shapeless, dirty white hunk of chalk. Pushing away the delicate strands of Queen Anne's Lace, I tried to make out the inscription, but it was impossible. The next marker was in slightly better shape; though the name and dates were illegible, it was still actually tombstone shaped. A nebulous blob perched on top of it, and I presumed it had once been an angel because there were so many of them all over the cemetery. The next few markers were also unreadable, topped with crumbling, but still recognizable, lambs. I wondered if this was a special burial area for farmers. Walking along while swatting away mosquitoes, I noticed some graves in better repair, each with a lamb sitting serenely on the crest of the headstones. I could make out their perky little ears, now rounded by the elements; their legs curled up under rounded bellies, four cloven hooves barely peeking out from beneath. *Maybe it was a section for shepherds?*

The next grave also had a lamb-and an intact epitaph. I read it and then had to re-read it a few more times because I just couldn't comprehend it. The grave was for a baby who was only three days old. Profound sorrow washed over me. I felt nauseous...*how was it possible*? I fell back in the grass alternately gazing at the fluffy clouds as though they were Angel Lambs in the sky, staring at the placid little lamb on the headstone, still in disbelief. Finally, I sat up, wondering what the baby had died of, whether they'd had brothers and sisters, and what the parents felt like when it happened. I started to cry again. Without thinking about what I was doing, I automatically brushed leaves and dirt off the base of the grave with my hands, picked some of the wildflowers and gently laid them there.

Eventually, I got up, taking a few tentative steps towards my bike, but felt compelled to go back to look at the rest of the graves. Even now, I don't know why I did or what I was expecting to see, but I truly was not prepared for more deceased infants and children... and there were several of them. I went from grave to grave looking at two, three, four, five, and six-year-old children; stillborn babies, and juvenile victims of Diphtheria, Scarlet Fever, Influenza and Whooping Cough. Then, the staggering reality hit me. Death wasn't only for old people, babies and children died on a regular basis, not just here, but *all over the world, and throughout time.*

I started weeping so deliriously, I could barely breath.

> *The firstborn offspring of our love*
> *Has safely winged its flight above*
> *Sweet little bud for earth too fair*
> *Hath gave to Heaven to blossom there*
> *Sleep on sweet babe and take thy rest*
> *God called thee home he thought it best*

** ** **

At the age of nine, I was no stranger to death, which in hindsight, is probably why I was so obsessed with the cemetery to begin with. I already knew animals could die suddenly. One sunny, late spring afternoon in Upstate New York, when I was four, my favorite dog and constant companion, Silkie, had been run over by a motorcycle on the rural road where we lived. The young man who hit him and his sobbing girlfriend knocked on our door, holding him gently, handing him over to my father like a tragic offering. My grief manifested immediately as hysteria. I hugged his limp body, his black button nose was still wet, and his corpse was still warm, keening like a Banshee.

In November of that same year, I was playing contentedly on the swing set in the yard, wearing my red parka because it was chilly and starting to rain. As I sang nursery rhymes to myself, my mother came out of the kitchen in tears. Scooping me off the swing, she told me President Kennedy had just been shot. She carried me to the living room couch just in time to watch an emotional Walter Cronkite announce on live television that the president had died.

At eight, I'd taken a beautiful young tabby cat in from the street and convinced my mother to let me keep her. Every night, Silversides slept with me all cuddled up and purring. She followed me around all day like a dog and I adored her. But when she gave birth to a single kitten, for some reason my mother wouldn't let me keep them both in the house, even though I begged. She put a box on the porch and told me to keep them out there. I was afraid that our neighbor's dog Pickles, who was known to hunt small prey, including cats, would attack them. Filled with anxiety over the situation, I could barely sleep each night, thinking about them outside, completely defenseless. On my way to school one morning, I noticed what I thought was a mouse laying on the brownstone steps near our front gate. Stooping down, I recoiled in horror when I realized it was the back half of the two-week-old baby kitten. Through a blur of tears, I saw that it had been severed in half. Its perfect tiny feet with their barely-walked-upon pads and miniscule, little tail were perfectly intact. I could see intestines. Reeling in agony, I vomited before collapsing on the step next to it, howling.

Brucie, one of the kids who lived in the house across the street next to the junkyard, stopped at the gate when he saw me crying. He looked at the kitten, informing me that his dog Pickles had run into the house with a bloody snout. Then he started jeering in a singsong, "My dog ate your kitty!" over and over before chomping his teeth, licking his lips, and heading up the street.

I ran into the house sobbing so inconsolably that it took a few minutes for my mother to understand what had happened. Shrugging, she said it was *nature* and sent me off to school. Numb with grief, I walked to school like an automaton. I still have no idea how I made it through that day, or the days that followed.

That summer, we rented a beach house in Groton for the weekend. Because of what had happened to the kitten, I was wildly anxious over my mother's nonchalance at leaving Silversides locked out of the house for the weekend. I pleaded endlessly to let me bring her along, and finally, my mother caved. The sunny weekend was fun, all sandcastles, sunburns, wave, jumping, and board games at night. But Silversides disappeared on Sunday afternoon as we were getting ready to go home. She didn't turn up after a full search of the house, so I walked around the yard, calling for her, shaking her cat treats, and growing increasingly alarmed.

After about fifteen minutes, my mother decided we had to leave… even though our house was less than forty minutes away, even though it was midafternoon and we had no plans for that evening, even though she knew how much I loved that cat. Facedown in the boot of the station wagon, I sobbed silently, my shoulders heaving. In a macabre moment of synchronicity as we were leaving Groton, my mother pointed out the shipyard where a new submarine was being built, the USS Silversides. *She actually said the name.* I cried even harder until I couldn't anymore.

Not too long after that, my beloved Grandma Pauline came to visit. A few days after she arrived, she collapsed in the middle of a supermarket, with my three younger siblings and me in tow. I remember waiting for what seemed like an eternity in the store's tiny office, listening to the buzz of the fluorescent lights as the manager tried to contact my mother, who was at work. My brother, sisters, and I were all crammed onto a broken down maroon Naugahyde couch with chrome railings, the type that would be in a train station or maybe a barbershop. I heard the ambulance siren as it pulled up to the store while my five-year-old twin sisters wailed along with it. I tried to calm them, I was the oldest, but started disassociating at that moment. I have no recollection of going home or who brought us there, my mother had apparently gone straight to the hospital, or for the rest of that afternoon, nor of that entire evening. The next time I saw my grandma was in a coffin at the funeral parlor. I was deeply disturbed that her ever-present fire engine red lipstick and nail polish had somehow been translated into a "tasteful" light pink. To me, that was an abomination, an erasure of who she was. I kissed her cheek just before the coffin lid closed. It felt cold, solid as a stone, and it wasn't scented with her Coty powder and her old-fashioned rouge. At the time, there was no such thing as grief counseling for children.

> *My life in infant days was spent*
> *While to my parents I was leant*
> *One smiling look to them I gave*
> *And then descended to the grave*

** ** **

Finally, the tears ran out and I caught my breath. The air around me was still. Emotionally exhausted, I stood up tentatively, once again ready to leave. But then I spotted yet another a lamb, this time lying on the ground, partially obscured by weeds. Like the others, it was weatherworn. It resembled a foot long, white marble loaf of bread, but it's innocent, placid face, trusting eyes and little delicate ears were fully intact. The stone it had once slept on was right behind it. I tried to re-settle the lamb for a very long time, but due to the way it had broken off and the elemental erosion, it kept tumbling to the ground. It happened over and over; I replaced it obsessively. I grew increasingly distressed, the lamb couldn't stay there on the ground, it needed to be *protected*. I held it in my arms for a while, rocking it, before heading back over to my bike. Tenderly, I wrapped the lamb securely in a red bandanna to keep it safe. Nestling it into the plastic basket mounted on the handlebars, I peddled home on autopilot.

I ditched my bike by throwing it down in the yard, something I never did because it was new and beautiful, and I wanted to keep it nice, before dashing up the stairs to the bedroom I shared with my sisters. I cradled the lamb in one elbow like a baby and wanted to sit it comfortably on my pillow. Suddenly, it became clear to me that I had just stolen part of a grave. As a kid who'd watched the horror movies on *Chiller Theater* religiously since the age of four, I fully understood that grave robbing was bad, it was a crime, and now I was afraid I'd go to jail. I needed time to think.

As I lifted up the old floral bed skirt, tucking the lamb in under my bed to hide it, the twins, Eddie and Meg, entered the room. Their curiosity was piqued by my covert action. They demanded to know what the big secret was, so I told them the whole story as I unwrapped the lamb for a viewing. They gasped in unison, eyes widening like the anxious, pleading emoji face. I let them touch it, and after a while, Eddie asked what I was going to do with it. I admitted that I had no idea.

> *We loved this tender little one*
> *And would have wished her stay*
> *But let our Father's will be done*
> *She shines in endless day*

Along with all the rest of the neighborhood kids, we were allowed out until dark in the summertime. Each night around nine o'clock, the mothers called their children home in unison. Dinner was Mom's homemade chili poured over macaroni, which stretched the meal substantially as well as inexpensively for four growing kids. As usual, the conversation was lively and chaotic, all of us talking over each other, interspersed with jokes we'd heard at school and merciless teasing, with some under-the-table kicking and dog, feeding mixed in. And then, the mood changed swiftly.

Even at the age of five, Meg was a self-righteous snitch.

She caught my eye judgmentally, like a middle-aged church lady, before announcing,

"Mom! Pleasant stole a lamb from Indian Hill today!"

Rising from the table, my mother flung the screen door open, peering into the back yard. I routinely brought home so many animals, fledglings and baby squirrels that that had fallen from their nests, several stray cats, a guinea pig, that she naturally assumed there was a live lamb frolicking around the yard. Standing at the door, she regarded me sternly with her piercing sea green eyes.

"Is this true... you took a lamb? Where is it?"

"It's under her bed!" Meg yelled, "*She stole it from a grave!*"

Mom had a volatile, mercurial temper. We never knew what to expect; she could go from calm and normal to *really* scary in no time. Her voice rising sharply, she ordered me to get the lamb. Bolting out of my chair, I took the stairs three at a time, both up and down. My face felt hot, and I trembled as I sat at the table again, unwrapping the bandanna, placing the lamb on the table so she could see it.

"Wow, *cool*!" Charlie proclaimed in awe.

Voice shaking with rage, my mother demanded I return it to Indian Hill immediately. Because it had been dark for well over an hour, and I was scared to go to the graveyard at night, I asked tentatively, hopefully, "Can I go in the morning?"

"*Right now!*" she ordered.

I didn't dare disobey.

As I rolled my bike down the porch stairs, the air closed around me so thick with stifling humidity that I felt like I was suffocating. Riding up to the corner, I noticed that Cross Street Market was closed, and all the neon was off, so it definitely must've been after ten. Vine Street was deserted with hardly any lighting. I'd never been there at night except for riding in my mom's car. Filled with trepidation, I pedaled as hard as I could. I wasn't sure whether or not I'd be punished, but at this point, it didn't even matter. Because my mother was so furious, I felt terrible and deeply ashamed. I was so sorry for the lonely, broken lamb and the little baby whose grave it had fallen from, but she hadn't even given me a chance to explain why I took it. I realized that it needed to go home to its rightful owner, even if it just had to lie in the grass near it, as it had for such a long time.

For some reason, the formidable wrought iron cemetery gates were open; I thought for sure they'd be locked. They looked ominous, as they did in all the horror movies I watched, but I sailed right through them, pretending it was daytime. A few yards beyond the gates, there was an intense explosion of thunder and simultaneously, the heavens opened up, pelting rain with such force it felt like nails driving into my entire body. My long thick hair was plastered to my face, and I was momentarily blinded from the rain rushing into my eyes. Intuitively, I headed in the direction I knew so well, my back tire leaving a wake in the same way a boat would. The air smelled of ozone; with each sheet lightening flash, the larger monuments appeared luminous. Pausing for a moment, I counted the seconds between the thunderclaps and lightening to see if I could calculate how far away the storm was. They were simultaneous, meaning the cloudburst was directly overhead.

Completely soaked, I continued riding with my head down, trying to keep the rain out of my face by leaning into the handlebars. When lightening hit, I passed mausoleums and trees I recognized, but the entire park was pitch dark between the lightning strikes. After a while, I had no idea where I was.

Stopping again, I planted my feet firmly on the ground, attempting to get my bearings. The gravel paths were built around the hill in level concentric circles, but the storm was so frightening and disorienting, I couldn't figure which side I was on *or* if I'd been going up or down. The chapel was the largest structure on the property, but in the dark it was impossible to locate the bell tower, and I needed to see it to know where I was. Dread set in, followed by primal fear. My breathing was shallow and rapid. I was hyperventilating and sick to my stomach. I'd been nervously chewing the inside of my left cheek since passing the market and could now taste blood flooding onto my tongue. *I should go back to the front gates…where are they?*

I forged ahead without any concept of how long I'd been in the graveyard. The rain wasn't letting up, my clothing felt like weights on my limbs and my thighs burned from pedaling. Physically and emotionally exhausted, shivering with terror, I knew I had to get out. I braked hard, reaching into the plastic basket; which had filled up like a pond. After freeing the lamb from the drenched bandanna, I continued pedaling blindly, zigzagging wildly from steering one-handed because my other arm was holding the lamb close to my body. When I sensed I was near the area where I'd found the lamb, I lobbed it as hard as I could towards the place where I hoped the graves were, without stopping. Sobbing, I made a sincere promise out loud, yelling into the darkness: *I'll come back in the morning and take you to your grave.*

At long last, the gates loomed before me, and I passed through them on the way to safety. The downhill momentum almost wiped me out as I hung a quick, jerky right on Vine Street, but like the lamb, I too was finally going home. The rest of the night was a blur. I don't remember getting home, falling asleep, or what, if anything, my mother said to me the next morning. In fact, I don't recall her talking about the incident *ever again.* The entire event, from the moment I spotted the graves to the second I flew through the cemetery gates in the dead of night seemed like a nightmare or a horrible hallucination.

Grabbing a Pop Tart and eating it cold, I headed to Indian Hill as soon as I could. Circling around the familiar paths, I spotted all my favorite monuments. The grass was so dry it was as though there hadn't been a raging electrical storm just a few hours ago. After three separate passes through the property, it dawned on me that I didn't have any idea where the section with the children's graves were... *or if they were really there.*

For days, I'd search endlessly without locating it. Wondering if I was going crazy, I started believing that I'd imagined the whole thing, but all my siblings assured me I did not, and they had actually seen and touched the lamb.

> *We had a little treasure once*
> *He was our Joy and pride*
> *We loved oh perhaps too well*
> *For soon he slept and died*

Over fifty years later, on a brief trip to Middletown, the first time I'd been back since leaving in the early 1970s, I returned to Indian Hill. It was a late afternoon in June, and aside from the fact that cemetery had grown considerably, it was exactly as I remembered it. The grand old trees still watched over my favorite monuments, which I located easily, as if by instinct. The lush, verdant grounds were meticulously cared for. The smell of recently mown grass combined with the floral arrangements and bouquets laid on the graves really brought me back. It was a unique fragrance, much different than the graveyards I'd visited anywhere else, even in other parts of New England. It was the scent of my childhood: the fleeting, simple joys and the enduring complex traumas, most of them, like a tiny corpse at rest beneath a stone lamb, deeply buried.

SEASON OF THE WITCH

The year my best friend Joan and I turned thirteen, we started keeping extensive journals, figuring that since we were now teenagers, we'd *finally* have something worth writing about. As The Shangri-La's put it, that something was love: L-U-V. I pictured the word as an eleven-story high casino sign in Las Vegas, spelled in poison green neon capital letters, a monumental beacon in an homage to Teenage Lust. Joan and I were ripe and ready for it: two nubile death-traps, gamey with jailbait.

In the early seventies, we were drunk on LUV-Free Love, Peace And Love, not to mention Love's Baby Soft cosmetics and Maybelline's roll-on Kissing Potion… yes, that was *really* what it was called. They came in "mouthwatering" flavors like luscious Strawberry, Honey Orange and, especially apropos for our virginal needs, Cherry. Our lips were dripping wet and drenched in promise; we were dying to be kissed.

The way Joan and I envisioned it, LUV was 18-22 years old, tall, and lanky. He'd have a long shag and wear tight patched jeans; hopefully, he'd be in a band. Blond, blue-eyed Tom, the neighborhood ice cream man fit the bill pretty well. He had a battered acoustic guitar with a Macrame strap stashed behind the driver's seat. Each time we heard the tinkling metal bells mounted on the roof Tom's truck, Joan and I would run into the street all Pavlovian in our cut-off denim hot pants and flimsy gauze halter tops. The younger kids had already gathered expectantly, glaring at us indignantly as Tom skipped over the line, handing us our Rocket Pops first. They were so pissed they didn't even notice that Joan and I got our frozen goodies for free…or that when the crowd dispersed, we'd disappear into the truck to hide on the floor kneeling between the freezers, smoking a jay with Tom.

As autumn approached, I'd learned that the word *triskaidekaphobia* meant "fear of the number thirteen." Unfortunately, most of the would-be Love Gods that Joan and I lusted after definitely had that fear. Life grew complicated and took on an air of espionage as we strove to be mature, mysterious, urban sophisticates.

We rearranged our lives in our pursuit of older dudes. Instead of rushing home from seventh grade to pull down the shades and watch *Dark Shadows* with half the neighborhood, we'd linger at O'Rourke's Diner, smoking Marlboros (the tough, worldly, hippie-fox brand) and drinking black coffee, which we absolutely hated, but God!, it looked *so* grownup. Sufficiently wired, we'd hit the Fashion Post boutique, trying on all sorts of groovy clothes, and then the Grand Union supermarket to shoplift the latest issue of *Star Magazine* and Maybelline Blooming Colors eye shadow compacts. I always wore Forest Green, because *Cosmo* said green eye shadow looked "wanton." Over dinner one evening, I asked my mother what the word wanton meant, and when she said "whorish." I knew with all my heart and soul that green was, indeed, the color of eye shadow I needed to express my true inner feelings.

Wanton-eyed and baby-faced, I waited as patiently as I could for what *Cosmo* termed a "torrid affair" to occur, but in those days of Free Love, alas… most older men didn't seem to notice willing, braless, thirteen-year-old virgins… not that it *mattered* at that point in my development, anyway; I was flat as a board. Joan and I had already succeeded in terrifying all the boys our own age. They didn't really fit in with our desires but still, it would've been a practical backup plan.

It was clear to both of us: we needed help in a big way.

Desperate, we turned to Occult Forces. With money saved from babysitting, I mail ordered a book called *Potions And Spells Of Witchcraft* from… I think it was an ad in the back of *Creem Magazine.* I put actual cash in the envelope because I wasn't gonna ask my mother to write a check; there was no way in *hell* want her to know I was becoming a witch. Joan and I started practicing witchcraft seriously, calling ourselves, only to each other, Pagans. We earnestly burned incense while cutting up bits of flannel fashioned into what we hoped were real mojo bags, filling them with hanks of hair, fingernail clippings, and coins. We buried a lot of shit in my backyard and at Indian Hill Cemetery. We'd stare for hours into candle flames, setting intentions and concentrating on our desires, usually David Bowie or Freddie Mercury, sewing up little felt dollies, sticking pins into their genital regions. We'd have sleepovers devoted to smoking an entire lid of raspy dirt weed before stripping naked, turning off the lights, and lying on the bed side by side for hours trying to Astral Project. Often, it seemed to work, though it was difficult to distinguish between a legit supernatural experience or the effect of the dope.

All of it went into our diaries: the crushes, the incantations, the makeup shoplifting missions, and the drug-inspired supernatural frenzies. We'd write detailed descriptions of what we wore every weekend on what we'd come to term our "Fox Hunts." We favored little antique satin lace-trimmed 1940s bed jackets, glitter platform wedgies (mine cost two weeks' pay and tips from an afterschool waitressing job) and tight-tight bell bottom jeans covered with Majik Marker doodles of dragons and unicorns. Mine had Queen, Jimmy Hendrix, Bowie and T-Rex lyrics written all over them in a loopy child's scrawl, every "I" dotted with a tiny star, *oh excuse me, I really meant to say Pentagram.*

Ultimately, with no magic other than nature involved, we both got our wishes and lost our virginity, and went on to become, at least for a time, homewreckers in earnest. Then, very suddenly, it seemed Joan and I were separated. I moved from Connecticut to Los Angeles, and we fell out of touch.

I spent the rest of my teens immersed in the early LA punk scene and most of my twenties touring in my all-girl band, The Screaming Sirens. We all had parttime boyfriends on the road, They were either in the bands we toured with or lived in some town we played in, sneaking out for a night of passion that usually took place in the back of our tour van on top of our amps, which had been made into a bed by covering them in filthy moving blankets.

By my mid-twenties, the way of life I'd aspired to as an underage floozy had grown tiresome. Even though I was still lookin' for love, I was pretty sick of bars, parking lots, motel rooms… and liars. A feral, defiant white-blonde punk rock bombshell, I was usually The Other Woman. On the few occasions I wasn't, I'd be some guy's Wild Last Hurrah before he settled down and married a *normal* chick who was a secretary. Had I been born a few centuries earlier, I definitely would've been paraded through town getting pelted by villagers throwing garbage, my head held high on my way to be burned at the stake. Life as a modern-day, man-eater hadn't turned out to be nearly as exciting as it had seemed before I'd taken a one-woman safari into The Jungle Of Lust.

A while back, I dug out an old, dusty box of my 1970s diaries, and with them, Joan's letters. I spent hours re-living our manic, desperate, truly *wanton* adolescent friendship. It was a union full of furtive notes passed in class with entire sentences underlined;

metallic, emerald-green nail polish a la Sally Bowles via Liza Minelli in *Cabaret*; Boone's Farm Ripple, LSD, dirt weed, and glam rock. There were intense hangovers while imprisoned in Saturday morning "study hall" (which was actually detention) and weekly sleepovers to watch *The Midnight Special*, *In Concert*, and *Don Kirshner's Rock Concert*.

Joan and I shared hallucinations on evenings spent marauding around various graveyards, went on crying jags together, and scored speed from the carnies and bikers who hung out at Coleman's Carnival. We cast spells, held candlelight seances, made dramatic entrances and exits, and routinely engaged in screaming matches with our single mothers. Entire afternoons were devoted to writing letters to "our" inmate J.R., whose Canton, Ohio prison address I'd also found in the back of *Creem Magazine*. Initially, J.R. (who was incarcerated for possession of weed, a *single joint*, I seem to recall) seemed hot and dangerous to us, but the letters he'd send back were polite, protective, and big brotherly in tone, as though he could sense through the mail that we were a couple of *little girls* with slutty aspirations. It's beyond impossible to estimate the amount of hours Joan and I spent listening to the Bowie, Mott The Hoople, Led Zeppelin, Iggy, New York Dolls, and Lou Reed albums we'd shoplifted from The Meriden Mall.

Down on the very bottom of the box was a paperback book Joan had given to me for my fourteenth birthday, *How To Become A Sensuous Witch: Spells, Rituals And Recipes For A Livelier Love Life By Abragail And Valaria*.

The well-loved cover featured a sultry sorceress with overly-plucked eyebrows, hot pants, and square-heeled lace-up boots posed fetchingly near a bubbling cauldron. I hadn't seen Joan in almost thirty years, but the book was still scented with her sandalwood oil, and by that alone, I could conjure her up.

Closing my eyes, she stands before me in a shoplifted silver Lurex tube-top and cut-off Levi's. Her thick, hip-length, Beautiful Breck Girl blonde hair shimmering, she's daring me to take another hit off the joint she's brandishing while she tosses her head, weaves around a bit on her platforms, dancing in all her teenage glory to our favorite song: Donovan's *Season Of The Witch.*

HAUNTED GARAGE

It was the summer of 1975 and as a recent transplant to Los Angeles, I was all about going to the beach. My constant companions were two guys I'd become really close with just days after arriving on my sixteenth birthday. I'd gone to a Queen concert at the Santa Monica Civic Auditorium; it was my first solo journey in search of rock 'n' roll in my new city. I took the bus there wearing a tattered 1940s evening gown with big sparkly sequins braided into my ass-length henna orange hair. A handsome, silver-haired man in the row in front of me handed me a joint, and it took a few seconds to realize it was Tony Curtis! I couldn't believe I was getting wasted with one of my favorite movie stars... *Welcome To Hollywood!*

Though his weed was potent and he was utterly charming, I got distracted by two guys walking down the aisle. One was dressed head-to-toe in white, with a neon orange Bowie shag. The other was shirtless in a floor-length cape and black satin pants. They looked so fucking cool coming down the aisle that I borrowed a pen from Tony Curtis, got a matchbook out of my antique beaded purse, and scrawled my number accompanied by a drawing of a miniature Saturn and some tiny Bowie lightning bolts. With that, I figured my message would pique their curiosity:

Aladdin Sane, you cosmic orgasms: CALL ME.

With the aim of a star pitcher, I threw it towards their seats just as the lights faded down for the show. Somehow, they caught it and called me the next day, grabbing the receiver from each other for the entire hour we spoke.

Their names were George and Paul; they were my age, and we started hanging out constantly. Both of them lived in West LA, near the beach, with their moms. Since I lived farther inland, mostly we'd meet in Westwood, which was the halfway point. We became a trio, partners in crime. We were into typical teenage trouble: hanging out in record stores and pizza places for hours, standing in the parking lots of liquor stores, convincing legal adults to buy us beer. We'd also dropped acid to stay up for days at a time and occasionally engaged in a little Vandalism Lite when we got antsy. Usually, we'd end up at Paul's house to get even more high before listening to Bowie for hours at a stretch. Eventually, I became George's first serious girlfriend.

A little later on, after they formed The Germs, George changed his name to Pat Smear and Paul became Darby Crash. One afternoon, during the drunken insanity unfolding as The Damned did an in-store appearance at Bomp Records, I got The Germs their first gig at the tiny black box Orpheum Theater. The Germs opened for The Nerves, The Weirdos, and The Zeros, and their set was absolute chaos… but I digress.

During summer vacation, we'd go to the beach together every day. The way it worked was: they'd call me and tell me to get on the bus at a certain time. I'd hop on the No.83 down Wilshire Boulevard and either or both of them would be stationed on a bus bench along the route, waiting for me to pop my head out the window and tell them to get onboard. Like my apartment, the elderly bus also lacked air conditioning, but it never mattered. I was on my way to spend the entire day with my favorite boys at the ocean.

George and Paul always hung out at Station 26, the "cool beach" where all the *loadies*, the seasoned surfers and the younger Z-Boys skaters all hung out. They'd catch waves among the submerged pilings that were the only remnant of the amusement park that had once been called POP, short for Pacific Ocean Pier. Station 26 was located in Ocean Park, but all the locals called it Dogtown. It was about three quarters of a mile south of the Santa Monica Pier, near Venice, which in those days was a rough neighborhood, so there were hardly ever any families or tourists. Most of the lifeguards on duty turned a blind eye to everyone openly passing joints around or day-drinking the beer that was barely concealed in paper bags. Once in a while, one or two of them of them even joined in.

One steamy July morning when the boys called, I had chores to do for my mom, so I told them I'd meet them at Station 26. I got off the bus on Lincoln near Bay Cities Italian Deli, deciding to take a shortcut. In those days, the side streets of Ocean Park would've been absolutely charming if they weren't so thoroughly dilapidated. They were full of ramshackle 1920s beach shacks crammed together tightly, faded pastel paint peeling off the wooden siding from decades of baking in the sun. The alleys were so narrow, it was clear they'd been built in the days before women had the right to vote. The only car that would've been able to fit in the doll house-sized garages lined up on the pothole-strewn pavement was a Model T Ford.

Wandering down an alley towards the shore, I noticed a hand-scrawled sign tacked to a telephone pole that said Garage Sale with an arrow. Always a sucker for vintage clothes, which weren't even called that yet, of course, I followed the arrow. Like a treasure hunt, there were more signs every few feet, posted on notepad-sized pieces of paper, so I walked farther down the alley, in the direction the arrows pointed.

One of the garages had a bunch of heavy furniture sitting on the asphalt in front of it. There were big, throne-like chairs and hutch cabinets with fancy brass pulls. They were antiques that looked like they were made of ebony or walnut. The garage door was wide open, so I called out, "Is this the sale?"

There was no answer. I tried again, a little louder. After a while, a muffled voice called back, instructing, "Come in."

The moment I entered the garage, I was blind. The midday summer sun was so bright my eyes didn't have a chance to adjust to the dark.

"Hi, do you guys have any old clothes?" I asked as loudly as possible.

Again, no answer.

Taking another step inside, I banged into a sharp corner, maybe a coffee table, hitting it so hard with my bare shin that I felt a trickle of blood running down my leg. I knew there'd be a huge, raised bruise with a severe scrape in the center. As my eyes adjusted to the pitch black, I realized I was standing in a sea of furniture. The garage was so packed that old fashioned chairs were stacked on top of each other, flanking the walls all the way up to the ceiling. Threadbare fainting couches with scrolling Victorian woodwork cozied up to Pembroke tables, fancy demi-lunes with metal latticework and glamourous 1930s vanities. Dressers topped by Italian marble slabs sat majestically next to tufted foot stools, hat racks and a variety of brass-trimmed steamer trunks that looked like they'd survived the sinking of The Titanic, The Lusitania and The Andrea Doria combined.

Then, so faintly that I thought I was imagining it, I heard Jazz Age big band music playing a foxtrot. It sounded like a scratched 78 rpm record playing through one of those old-time *His Master's Voice* Victrola phonographs. I loved those old gramophones, the kind with the big-stamped steel flower horns. My father had one when I was little; it was always special treat when he let me let me crank it up.

> *You left me sad and lonely*
> *Why did you leave me lonely?*
> *For here's a heart that's only*
> *For nobody but you*

I hadn't seen any vintage phonographs among all the other stuff, so squeezing carefully through the maze of furnishings, I headed towards the place the music seemed to come from, thinking maybe the sale continued in a yard behind the garage. As I stood at the back wall, the lilting foxtrot slowed down grotesquely before fading away altogether as the spring-driven motor died down.

Momentarily, the silence was replaced by the nearly-inaudible, but unmistakable, sound of the grooves on an old record skipping and popping. *Someone had changed the record.* A military march played as the needle sizzled up to full volume on the old shellac. I patted the wall to see if I could find the entrance to the backyard. I felt a velvet curtain, and it occurred to me there might be a doorway behind it. To get my bearings, I briefly turned around, catching sight of the front of the garage. Somehow, the blazing sunlight appeared to be awfully far away. As the march played on, something seemed... off. The back of my neck prickled, and goosebumps rose on my skin.

Suddenly, two black arms ending in white-gloved hands thrust out from behind the curtain just above my shoulders, on either side of my head. Too shocked to move, I stood perfectly still as the flood of adrenalin hit my system. The arms seemed really long, perhaps about twenty inches from just above the elbow to the fingertips. The glove on the right held a conductor's baton properly, lightly between the thumb and forefinger, waving it elegantly through the air in perfect time with the tempo of the march. Thoughts raced through my head, piling up on top of one another like a multi-vehicle crash on the freeway.

Was it a puppet? A mechanized mannequin?

Frozen in place, I was in a trance, as though I was having a night terror. The only part of me that moved were my eyes, darting wildly from side to side, watching the surreal movement of the Conducting Hands. They were so close I could see a golden cufflink in each crisply starched cuff and three finely hand-stitched seams on the top of each glove....*Just like Mickey Mouse,* I thought wildly.

I couldn't comprehend what was happening... but the second I noticed the black hair growing on the wrists between the cuff and the glove, I realized with a nauseating wave of horror that the conducting hands belonged to a *human.* Bolting immediately with a second rush of adrenalin, I crashed into, and clambered on top of, most of the furniture trying to get outside.

Out in the alley all sweaty and panting, waiting for my legs to stop trembling in the harsh glare of the sun, I wondered what the hell had just happened. I had no idea how long I'd been inside the garage.

Finally, as my adrenaline rush subsided, I got my shit together and headed towards Station 26.

George and Paul were sitting on threadbare beach towels printed with palm trees and setting suns. As they spotted me, they shook their salty wet hair like dogs, droplets flying off Paul's neon orange Bowie shag, taking a little of the hair color with them.

"What took you so long?" George asked, rising to give me a kiss.

I knew without a doubt they'd be fascinated with the story if I told it, but I was too mentally and emotionally exhausted to even attempt it. Not to mention there was also the *highly* probable chance that once they heard it, both of them would demand to be taken back to the garage immediately. Somehow, neither of them seemed to notice the bleeding scratches on my arms from scaling the furniture… *or* the huge egg-like swelling on my right shin and the thick rivulet of dried blood dripping all the way down to my ankle; it had formed a giant crusty pool on the top of my foot.

"Oh you *know*," I shrugged, taking a long hit off the joint that'd been handed to me, "The bus was running late."

MOVIES 'TIL DAWN

Back in the days before cable television, it was common for local television channels to run old motion pictures all night long. As the Movie Capital Of America, Los Angeles was a goldmine in this arena. There was always an arbitrary grab bag of movies. You never knew what would come on, but it was practically a guarantee that even if you watched just once a week, you'd get a wide and varied education in film history. My favorite was *Movies 'Til Dawn on* KTLA Channel 5. Most nights, their selections were so disparate, it didn't make any sense whatsoever. There was no curating whatsoever; it was like an employee at the station had a few shots, closed their eyes, and randomly picked the movies by playing Film Cannister Roulette.

In the late 1970s through the mid '80s, they'd run everything from classics like *Rebel Without A Cause* or The *Postman Always Rings Twice* interspersed with suspense films like *Play Misty For Me* or *Hush, Hush Sweet Charlotte.* Some nights, there'd be 1960s socio-dramas like *To Sir With Love*, starring Sidney Poitier and rock icon Michael Des Barres as a hot Cockney hooligan followed by beachy B movies like *How To Stuff A Wild Bikini* and ridiculously bad 1950s horror films such as *Plan 9 From Outer Space* or *The Brain That Wouldn't Die.* It was the perfect late-night entertainment for anyone, who, like my friends and me, had gotten home from a party or club wasted on beer, weed, and prescription pills purchased from shady characters on Hollywood Boulevard.

It was during these late-night film binges hat I had two paranormal experiences with my life-long bestie Kid Congo Powers. Before he became a famous guitarist with iconic bands like The Cramps, The Gun Club and Nick Cave and The Bad Seeds, he was my regular partner in crime. We'd take Greyhound buses across the country to hang out on New York's Lower East Side, going to CBGB and Max's Kansas City. We were also roommates at two different LA punk houses. We shared a room at 909 Palm Drive (known in the early '70s scene simply as "909") and also at Disgraceland. Born ten days apart in 1959, we'd celebrate our birthdays together. We loved all the same music, books and films, and our shared surreal sense of humor was always on the same page. One night at 909, we were frying on acid when teenage songwriter Kari Krome called The Runaways' producer Kim Fowley and told him to come over. Horrified, Kid and I *really* didn't want to see him… so we took the entire knife drawer out of the kitchen cabinet and absconded to our room, barricading the entrance with our beds. When Kim arrived, he banged on our door, loudly demanding to be let in, while Kid and I slid everything from butter knives to full-sized butcher's meat cleavers through the cracks in the doorjamb, hollering at him to stay away…. *but I digress.*

After we got evicted from 909 in 1977 and a year before Kid and I moved into Disgraceland, he had a room, well, a closet *pretending* to be a room, at The Wilton Hilton. The rambling two-story Craftsman house is now a fully restored bed and breakfast but was also a notorious Hollywood punk house. The kings of The Wilton Hilton were Tomato Du Plenty and Tommy Gear of the LA scene's most revered but most under-recorded band, The Screamers.

To Kid and me, Tomata and Gear were *old*, as in their late twenties, and we idolized them because of their startling looks. They wore shit like real 1950s leather jackets festooned with chains, antique straightjackets from a mental asylum, and both had gravity-defying hair that stood straight up, courtesy of their hairdresser roomie Chloe Pappas. The Screamers also had an impressive rock 'n' roll pedigree. They'd had a band in Seattle called The Tupperwares, along with Eldon Hoke (the given name of a pre-Mentors El Duce) and drummer Bill Reiflin, who later went on to play with Ministry, among others.

Tomata and Gear's most glamorous roommate was gorgeous redhead Fayette Hauser, a founding member of the licentious San Francisco based theatrical drag-cabaret The Cockettes. For a New York stint in the early '70s, Fayette and Tomata had a theatrical comedy troupe that played at places like CBGB with newly formed bands like The Ramones and Blondie, opening for them. At the time, both were still unknown local bands.

The Wilton Hilton had its own wild history, too. According to Tomata, in the 1920s it had once been the Hollywood love nest of William Randolph Hearst and his lifelong silent movie star mistress Marion Davies. During the 1930s, Paramount had used the house as a dormitory for their contract-player starlets. Apparently, in the early the 1960s, Pamela Des Barres' wild all-girl, all groupie band The GTO's lived there, followed by a Satanic cult who moved in during the early 1970s. This seemed to be confirmed by the perfect ritual circle burned into the hardwood floor in Gear's room…not to mention the fact that the downstairs neighbor's dog was constantly digging up cat skulls from the back yard.

When The Screamers moved in, the house was already super creepy. The walls on the staircase leading up to their second story apartment were painted flat black, with a large safe built in at the foot of the steps, topped by a framed blow-up of the cover of *Paris*

Match from August 5, 1962, proclaiming "Marilyn East Morte!".

Well into the wee hours one evening, Kid, Brad Dunning, who went on to become The Gun Club's drummer, our pal Chuck Fulton and I were hanging out at The Wilton Hilton, smoking insane amounts of weed and watching *Movies 'Til Dawn*. John Huston's darkly sexual psychodrama *Reflections In A Golden Eye* starring Elizabeth Taylor and Marlon Brando flickered across the screen of a tv set that'd been salvaged from the trash. Liz was in the midst of sauntering up the stairs nude when she paused to humiliate Brando, asking in supercilious whisper,

"Son, have you ever been collared and dragged into the street …and been thrashed by a naked woman?"

Just then, the commercial break interrupted. It was always ten straight minutes of deranged ads from local car dealer Cal Worthington.

"Heeeeere's Cal Worthington…and his dog Spot!" Once in a while, Spot was actually a dog, but he was often a tiger, hippopotamus, seal, or some other wild animal. Even though the ads were fun, especially when late-night viewers like us were wrecked on *hoochiewana*, making Jiffy Pop seemed like a better idea, so Kid and Chuck beat it into the kitchen.

Minutes later, while Brad and I watched Cal Worthington flying through the air with his feet strapped to the wings of an antique bi-plane, smoke drifted through the hallway. Realizing Kid and Chuck might be too stoned to manage the Herculean task of making instant popcorn, we headed to the kitchen. Things were under control, but the smoke in the hall was getting dense, so Brad and I made a safety check. The other rooms were fine; nothing out of the ordinary, but as soon as I opened the door to Gear's room, oily black smoke billowed out. Oddly, there were no visible flames or heat in the room, so I walked in. Through the clouds of black smoke, I checked the closet, nothing was burning. I could see the Dormer windows facing the street were all open. Taking a few steps towards them, I looked outside; the smoke wasn't coming from the street. Then it hit me: *none of the smoke was blowing out the window! How could this much smoke come from a room where nothing was burning?*

Creeped out from what I'd just witnessed, I returned to the hallway where Brad swore he'd just seen two white cats screeching around the corner from Gear's room before running down the stairs. Shaken, we went back to the room where *Movies 'Til Dawn* was on; Kid and Chuck cheerfully offered us Jiffy Pop still hot from the stovetop.

Discussing this episode years later, Brad and I went over every possible explanation for the smoke without coming up with anything logical. We knew The Screamers never owned cats. Once again, Brad said they were ghosts, but that they also looked "kind of opaque" so he thought they might've actually been real... until they faded out while trotting down the stairs. Finally, both of us connected the ghost cats to the circle burned into the floor of Gear's room... and all the feline sculls the neighbor's dog had dug up from the back yard.

** ** **

One night in late Fall of 1980, the moment Kid and I got home from The Whisky, we decided to drop acid. Because our house Disgraceland was located between Hollywood Boulevard and Sunset Boulevard at the corner of Selma Avenue in central Hollywood, it was within walking distance of all the bars on both streets, it was the perfect afterhours hang. As always, a few people were gathered in our living room, drinking and getting high. "Spinning Rock Boogie" by Hank C. Burnett was cranked up on my shitty Sears Roebuck stereo, and there was a new fifth of vodka on the battered coffee table. Before we got too messed up, Kid slipped into my room to return a call from Lux and Ivy, though it wasn't public knowledge yet, he'd left The Gun Club to join The Cramps.

By the time we made it back to the living room, we were already coming on to the LSD. Almost everyone had left except our old 909 roommate Dennis, who crashed at Disgraceland regularly; he made us cocktails and we turned on *Movies 'Til Dawn*, hoping for a horror movie. Our wish was granted, and the film was fantastic, not low budget cheesy, but not a classic, either. It was actually done very well. The acting was decent, and it looked like it was filmed on location at Arches Park in Utah. Unfortunately, I can't remember what it was called and have tried googling it for years, to no avail.

The plot revolved around a vacationing family whose car broke down somewhere in the desert near the spectacular, towering natural rock formations. They're out there in the middle of the wilderness for hours under the blazing sun with no other cars on the road, no civilization, and not even a gas station anywhere nearby. The hungry, sunburned kids are wailing; the family is running out of water. Finally, another motorist comes down the deserted road. It turns out to be a minister who somehow, I'm not entirely clear exactly *how* because I was blazing on acid at that point, the minister gets the car going or tows it back to his little town. Initially, the desert hamlet of Aselm appears to be a cheerful, smoothly running commune. To the viewer, it's instantly obvious it's a cult compound, but the grateful family doesn't notice until it's too late. There's some kind of clandestine Devil worship involved, and in the midst of the rituals, which are getting more intense by the second, there are quick flashing subliminal scenes from centuries ago of Puritan women on trial. Naturally, I assumed they were from Salem, Massachusetts, where so many women were accused of witchcraft. Because I was high and the scenes cut in and out so rapidly, it was difficult for me to tell if they were dreams, flashbacks, an actual time slip, or alternate universe type scenario.

It was at this point in the film that I started hearing real-life scratching sounds and almost inaudible whispers. They seemed to be coming from our driveway, but I wasn't a hundred percent sure. I knew implicitly that I wasn't hallucinating, but also didn't want to mention it to Kid... at least not *yet*.

As crazy as he could get when we were both wrecked, Kid often thought I overreacted to external stimuli when I was wasted on hallucinogens. To me, having extreme reactions to wild experiences was... *normal*. We'd tripped in a multitude of bizarre situations-graveyards, drive-in movies, the Harry Houdini Mansion... not to mention riding the ancient, rickety Thunderbolt Rollercoaster endlessly at Coney Island before taking the subway home and wandering down the post-apocalyptic hellscape of The Bowery at 3:30am. One time, higher than shit, we'd crashed a party at the notoriously haunted Hollywood Tower. The penthouse was packed, and all the lights were out, so it was dark and shadowy. The host had projected 1920s silent films onto the whitewashed walls. Each one featured humongous pythons in the jungle. They were ingesting large animals like sheep and antelopes in real time. It was horrific. Even with all the revelers in the darkened room, watching the carnage was unavoidable. It bummed me out so hard that I pushed my way through the crowd searching for the bathroom so I could flip on a light and change my mood. Opening what I assumed was the bathroom door, it turned out to be a closet. Besides the bare clothes rack, it was empty except for a white sack on the floor from which a live, and *really* large, boa constrictor leapt out vertically, striking at me. Screaming, I slammed the door immediately, pushing through the party aggressively, trying to locate Kid. As I rambled on breathlessly about the snake, he raised an eyebrow skeptically, and I could tell he thought I was embellishing what I'd seen until I dragged him through the crowd to show him.

In short, I needed to make absolutely sure that the voices and scratching noises were *real* before I asked Kid if he was hearing it too.

"Did you hear whispering?" Kid inquired somewhat hesitantly.

My eyes were glued to the television, watching scenes of witches on the gallows or being burned at the stake. I was so high it sounded as though Kid was talking in slow motion… or *backwards masking* his speech.

"Yeah…" I drawled without breaking my focus on the film. My reply sounded like there was an echo chamber in my head.

The racket from outside seemed to increase for a bit before stopping altogether. At one point, the windows actually rattled. Kid stepped outside for recon, but everything seemed normal, no raccoons on the trash cans; the sidewalk and our driveway were both deserted. When we heard giggling, Kid threw one of the windows open, discovering Lux and Ivy crouched on the side of the house, hands over their mouths trying to keep silent. Bursting into laughter over being discovered, they came in to visit. They'd been out there around a half hour, knew we were on psychedelics through eavesdropping, and had both wondered how long it'd take us to catch on.

Kid was able to converse with them, but I was so gone I could barely speak. I was fully engrossed with the film, which was reaching its dramatic conclusion. The father had somehow gotten his confiscated, and now repaired, car back. During an uprising in the compound, he'd managed to pile the family in, and they made an escape, with the cult members in hot pursuit, playing a wild game of chicken along the endless desert road.

The moment the family left the Devil worshippers in the dust, they whizzed by a road sign that read NOW LEAVING ASELM. The camera's point of view switched quickly, focusing on the car's rearview mirror, filled with the distorted image of the sign. In an instant, ASELM was replaced by SALEM, and that was how the movie ended.

In my drugged-out stupor, I'd gotten so wholly involved in the film that anything else going on in the living room, like Lux, Ivy and Kid blasting vintage rockabilly 45s and laughing uproariously, were obliterated. In my acid consciousness, I found the ending to be *profound:* ASELM/SALEM …like, wow, so *heavy,* right?

As the endless Cal Worthington commercials started up again, I stepped out onto the Disgraceland porch for a few moments of contemplation about the film I'd just seen, the witch trials that had been depicted, the Spanish Inquisition, and the early settler women that had been condemned as witches in the colony of Massachusetts. Though it might seem hard to believe, back in the early 1980s, Hollywood after dark was like a sleepy Midwestern town. After 10:00pm, the streets were deserted; the sound of crickets and the balmy evening air were peaceful. Nestling myself onto the incongruous baby pink porch swing and rocking gently, I enjoyed the silence, thinking about the film… until something strange caught my eye. There was a streetlight at the corner intersection, just a few feet away from where I sat, its hazy glow illuminating the street sign beneath it: Selma Avenue. Even though I'd seen that sign every fucking day I'd lived at Disgraceland, I had to look two or three times to make sure I was actually seeing what I *thought* I was seeing: ASELM, SALEM… SELMA.

GRAVEYARD GIRL

Breathing deeply, I opened my mouth opened wide, yearning to receive his essence, feeling him in my very core. This... thing we had together went on at least twice a week and lasted for years, from the late 1970s to the mid-1990s; it was a *ritual*. Around midnight, I'd steal through the unlocked gates of Hollywood Memorial Park, now known as Hollywood Forever Cemetery, heading directly to Douglas Fairbanks Junior's monument. Trotting the length of the magnificent reflection pool, my anticipation grew because I was about to commune with the star of *Robin Hood, The Thief of Baghdad, Zorro*. I needed his devil-may-care, swashbuckling, adventurous spirit... so I'd cram my *entire face* into the vents of his tomb, open my mouth as big as the Great White Shark on the *Jaws* poster, inhaling deeply until I almost passed out. I was trying my best to absorb his silent movie star DNA, hoping it would affect my genetic makeup by changing my chromosomes. Though I'd ingested copious amounts of controlled substances in my life, none were nearly as potent.

The vents on Douglas Fairbank's sarcophagus have been cemented shut for decades, and the cemetery gates are now padlocked at dusk, but in the '70s, you could just walk right in after dark, and several people did. Back then, before new owners bought the property and renamed it, the entire place was in such dire disrepair it looked like a set from a mid-sixties Hammer Films B Movie Vampire flick. All that was missing was Peter Cushing and Christopher Lee.

Not only were the main gates always carelessly left open at night, but the baroque wrought iron doors on the Edwardian era mausoleums were also rusted and hanging from their hinges; some had been pried off and lay on the ground. A few of the mausoleums had visible, and severely vandalized, coffins inside, surrounded by broken beer bottles and covered in "R13" spray paint tags from local gang The Rebels. Pre-1920s gravestones tilted at crazy angles due to settling ground; weeds grew rampant; the grass was rarely, if ever, mowed. Bouquets of weatherworn cheap plastic flowers and fading, shredded miniature American flags stood forlornly on the markers. A few pieces of statuary were missing hands, lyre harps or the tips of their angelic wings; others were defaced with graffiti.

In those days, the cemetery was an after-hours hot spot for juvenile delinquent punks like me: it was free to get in, no one carded you, and you could make all sorts of racket cause the neighbors weren't alive. I did more drugs and had more sex in the graveyard than I ever did in my house. I actually considered Hollywood Memorial Park my *bedroom*. My favorite spot for dead-of-night (pun intended) erotic encounters was the island monument. I'd bring my leopard print flannel sleeping bag, a handful of Quaaludes and a hot squeeze. Sometimes we'd simply pass out there, waking up as dawn broke.

I loved having human sex with the dead as voyeurs. I caroused on the markers for Tyrone Power, Cecil B. DeMille and on the marble floor underneath Rudolph Valentino's niche. Raised as a feminist, I avenged Fatty Arbuckle's abuse of silent film starlet Virginia Rappe by copulating on her grave, leaving her a paper cupful of Cold Duck and one of my earrings as an offering. Mel Blanc's head stone looks average except for the best, and most appropriate, epitaph ever: *That's All Folks*. Once I hooked up on it with a cute goth guy I'd just met at a punk show; he loved that I dragged him to a cemetery tryst when we were both on acid. After we finished our Loony Tunes Love Fest, the boy said, "What's Up Doc?" in a Bugs Bunny voice and I was certain he was *husband material*. But that was all folks…I never saw him again.

The following incident took place during the very rainy Spring of 1978. I'd just turned nineteen and was tripping my brains out on LSD. Pop-punk band The Mumps were in town from New York City. Darlings of the Lower East Side CBGB scene, The Mumps were led by the infamous Lance Loud, who'd come out on national television on the PBS show *An American Family*. I'd interviewed The Mumps for *Slash Magazine* and they'd just been on the cover of *Lobotomy: The Brainless Magazine*, a Xerox fanzine I did with my high school class-ditching pal Randy Kaye and our close buddy, photographer Theresa Kereakes.

Theresa was one of the only people in our crowd with a car, a little Honda that had recently transported a load of crazies up to San Francisco to see The Sex Pistols at Winterland. One night, Theresa, my roommate Kid Congo, guitarist of The Gun Club (and later, The Cramps, Nick Cave, etc.) and I took Mumps' bassist Kevin Kiley to get a whiff of Douglas Fairbanks.

We cracked bottles of illegally purchased Mickey's Big Mouth beer as we sloshed through the muddy, overgrown grass, showing Kevin our favorite gravesites. Though I was appalled that so many of them had been vandalized, I thought nothing of plucking Easter Lilies from the bouquets the living had left for their dearly departed. I loved fresh flowers and couldn't afford them. Kevin helped me gather up a big bouquet as we chanted repeatedly in a Katherine Hepburn voice,

"THE CALLA LILLIES ARE IN BLOOM!"

Somehow, I fell behind the group, stopping at a life-sized statue of a weeping woman, her hands covering her face. I watched in morbid fascination as the collected water from the recent rain slowly dripped through her fingers like tears, splashing onto the granite pedestal. Since I was so damn high, I wondered if this effect had been planned by the sculptor, though it was also entirely possible it was a hallucination… or a *miracle*.

Presently, I thought I heard a low whistle, but chalked it up to being freaked by the spooky statue, until I heard bushes rustling; seconds later there was another faint whistle and then footsteps. Stiffening in fear, I went as alert and still as a hunted doe. I tuned in on two men's voices mumbling but couldn't make out the words. They seemed very close by, and were *definitely* not wildlife, a ghost or a hallucination. With a chill, I felt their eyes on me and knew it wasn't my imagination, so I walked away swiftly, and as casually as possible, to find my friends.

"There's other people here," I said in a breathless whisper, "They're hiding, and I think they've been watching us…and…we should go…like *now!*"

Kid rolled his eyes. We'd taken acid together so many times, he knew I was prone to bizarre thoughts and obsessive behavior. Once, while in the throes of LSD inspired mania, I made him buy a box of Ritz Crackers. At my insistence, we spent hours carefully examining every cracker individually, *with a magnifying glass*, to see if they really had SEX stamped onto them as a form of subliminal seduction.

"You're just being paranoid," Kid said patiently.

"No, I *swear*!", I gasped, trying not to flip out. "We gotta get out of here!"

There was another loud whistle, and this time we all heard it, whirling around in unison.

A tall, heavy-set man appeared from behind one of the mausoleums. He had wild long black hair, crazy eyes and was brandishing a length of lead pipe. He ran towards us as a second guy in a leather jacket also armed with a pipe, closed in, coming from the area near the front gates.

"Run!" Kevin yelled.

Everyone took off, instinctively sprinting for the east wall of the cemetery bordering Van Ness Avenue, where Theresa had parked. Kid was already perched on top of the wall, extending his hand as I threw my bundle of Easter Lilies over before climbing up. Getting a boost from Kevin, I used the thick ivy to hold on, but it was slippery with dew. Though Theresa was last to scale the wall, she unlocked the car with miraculous speed. As we pulled out, the first thug grabbed the door Kid was closing, and with abnormal, probably Angel Dust powered-strength, kept it open until Theresa abruptly backed the Honda up, knocking him to the sidewalk.

Speeding south on Van Ness, the late model Impala the thugs drove followed us in hot pursuit. For nearly thirty minutes, we darted in and out of small, quiet side streets at high speed, trying to lose them but they tailed us so closely it was impossible.

Meanwhile, I was having a legit panic attack in the back seat because there were giant slugs crawling all over the lilies I'd stolen. There's almost nothing I hate more than slugs, they're so slimy, leech-like and disgusting. Snails are ok because they've got cute little shell houses on their backs, but slugs? *Nope!* As we lurched around corners, I started screaming, not at the situation, but from girly-girl Slug Panic. In phobic overdrive, I shoved every stalk that had a slug on it to Kevin, who, only to humor me, and probably to make me shut the fuck up, started stuffing them out the tiny, two-inch window vent, one by one. Lilies flew non-stop onto the Impala's windshield, making direct hits like floral missiles.

There were at least ten huge Calla lilies plastered to the glass and in hindsight, I'm reasonably sure the lack of visibility they created was the sole reason Theresa made it onto Melrose Avenue. She hung a left and with a squeal of tires, did a huge donut, driving illegally on purpose, hoping to attract the attention of the cops. Finally, we lost the Impala and jammed down the deserted street going ninety all the way to La Brea, heading north to Theresa's pad.

Completely shaken, we exited the car and gratefully entered her apartment. The Mumps' drummer Paul Rutner, who'd opted out of the cemetery excursion in favor of rest, was shocked when he saw our faces.

"What the hell happened to you guys?" he asked, adding without a single drop of irony,

"You're as white as ghosts!"

LUCKY FOUR-LEAF CLOVER

During the 1980s, my house Disgraceland was Hollywood Party Central. It was like a punk rock version of Las Vegas shrunk into a two-bedroom shotgun flat: one quarter of a 1920s stucco fourplex on a quiet side street in central Hollywood. We should've had a big billboard on the roof, but we didn't *need* one. Even though social media didn't exist, Disgraceland became internationally known because of articles that appeared in publications like *Rolling Stone*, *Spin*, *Slash Magazine*, *New York Rocker*, *NoMag* and *Flipside* plus a plethora of small, photocopied fanzines. Everybody was well aware of Disgraceland's debauched reputation: sex, drugs, rock'n'roll and of course, booze were on the menu twenty-four hours a day. One party blended into another for days...or weeks. My roommate Mike Martt of Tex & The Horseheads owned a big craps table that was never *out* of action; anyone who came over had to play dice: people bet with leather jackets, cowboy boots, amps, guitars; once, someone even bet their car. Then there was the time Mike forced a technician from the Department Of Water And Power to play with us before we allowed him access to turn off our electricity. We were all so obsessed with playing craps that if the phone rang, which it did constantly, everyone would do a quick roll of the dice *while it was ringing,* and the loser had to answer.

Our landline phone was a complete necessity, especially since we couldn't afford an answering machine. My roommate Iris Berry and I were such hardcore phone abusers that when she (finally) got her own line, we'd actually lay in bed calling each other's bedrooms collect, having half hour-long conversations even though we were fifteen feet down the hallway from each other!

The Disgraceland Hotline never stopped ringing *ever*...unless, of course, it was shut off. This was such a common occurrence, an almost *monthly* occurrence, that it was the bane of our existence. My name was on the phone bill, and it was never easy to round up everyone's share; it was, as Tom Waites once eloquently stated, "harder than Chinese Algebra". One time, a touring band stuck us with such an astronomical long-distance bill that it fucked us up for months. There was a continuous outstanding balance that never fully got paid, and that, combined with our consistently late payments, was apparently Ma Bell's Last Straw. The phone was dead when I picked up the receiver one morning (ok, it was actually 3:00pm, but that was *early* by Disgraceland standards) so I trotted up to a Hollywood Boulevard phone booth to waste a dime by pleading with them to turn it back on. No dice. The representative flatly refused unless I brought the $125.00 total we owed down to the office *in cash* before five o'clock. I offered the seventy-five bucks I had, but it was steadfastly turned down. Then the bitch informed me that once the phone was shut off, I'd also have to pay a huge deposit to have service restored.

The bill was such a large amount that I panicked...until I remembered my Aunt Clara's sterling silver dinner service. It was a full set for eight people: knives, forks and spoons, even butter knives and teaspoons, and each piece bore a hallmark. Since my right arm was loaded almost to the elbow with sterling bracelets, I figured my appraisal skills were pretty good; it had to be worth something substantial. Though I knew plenty of musicians who'd hocked their guitars and amps regularly, I'd never been in a pawn shop before, let alone hocked anything. Plus, the silver was An Heirloom. I debated whether or not I'd be able to pay the pawn ticket when the time came, and it was stressful. Yet I found myself getting dressed, stuffing the silverware, which was way heavier than I thought it would be, into a 1950s gold lame tote bag and going around the corner to the pawn shop, which was near my favorite witch shop, Panpipes.

The pawn shop was intimidating. A nondescript cinderblock building with a door covered in thick black metal rebar, it looked like an ideal place to murder someone and dismember the corpse without being caught. A gargantuan security camera was mounted over the entranceway and there was a greasy, well-worn button to press to get buzzed in. I suddenly felt like this was a bad idea but touched the button anyway and the door swung open. The guy at the counter looked like a biker or possibly a pro wrestler.

"Whatcha got for me honey?" he asked in a gruff, B Movie Criminal Accent while giving me the once over twice.

I dumped the cutlery onto the counter. He rolled his eyes as several forks clattered to the bare cement floor. Putting on one of those monocle thingies that jewelers wear, he sighed, barely examining the set before barking "pass". He drove the point home by picking up a dog-eared Playboy and licking his fingers as he paged through it, dismissing me.

Relieved to be out of there but dejected cause I needed cash, I wandered into The Panpipes for a little self-soothing. The air was always scented with Eau De Occult Shop: my nickname for the way all witchy shops smell, each store slightly different. It's a heady mix of incense and herbs, dusty old grimoires and the essential oils used to dress candles for spells. Statues of Goddesses and Gods from every conceivable pantheon were on display; tiny altars had been set up in nooks and crannies and there was a black velvet-lined display case packed full of magickal baubles like tiny Pentagram earrings and Triple Goddess pendants.

Perusing the jewelry selection just to daydream about everything I couldn't afford, my eyes were drawn the single piece of gold in the case. It was a stunning ring with an intricately carved horseshoe topped by a four-leaf clover. Obviously vintage, it was a beautifully crafted piece of Black Hills Gold that stood out so spectacularly it seemed to have a shimmering nimbus around it. First created in 1870 during The Gold Rush, Black Hills Gold is a unique type of jewelry made of different gold alloys: the standard yellow gold combined green and pink gold. The pieces usually portray grape clusters, leaves and vines; I'd never before seen a horseshoe or for that matter, a four-leaf clover. Each of the four leaves on the realistic-looking clover were green gold and I was enchanted.

The Voice popped into my head suddenly, commanding:

Get the ring, it will bring you luck!

The ring was still in the case, but my hand was already in my purse reaching for my wallet. As though I was in a trance, I asked the price-fifty bucks, and handed over the cash, without even trying it on. The clerk handed me the ring and I slipped it onto the second finger of my left hand, thanked the clerk and left the shop. The little brass bells attached to the door tinkled like audible fairy dust as I exited, closing the door softly behind me.

I walked about a block before stopping to admire the ring, holding my hand out at eye level like a giddy woman who'd just gotten engaged. The sun glinted off the leaves, illuminating every little vein. Each delicate detail in the horseshoe was realistic, down to the microscopic nail heads.

All of a sudden, reality slapped me hard as I felt the weighty bulk of the bag full of Aunt Clara's silverware: *now I couldn't pay the goddamn phone bill.* But The Voice had spoken.

The Voice wasn't something I experienced often, but when I did, I somehow knew it wasn't a thought of my own; it was clearly another person, I just couldn't see who it was. Somehow, this never unnerved me; I implicitly understood that I had to listen carefully and either relay the message or do what it said.

The first time I heard it, I was four. We lived in a Revolutionary War era farmhouse in Upstate New York, way out in the sticks. I was sitting on a braided rug, watching TV in The Little Room, my playroom that faced the woods. The Voice was a man hollering at me, saying our barn, which was on the opposite side of our property, was on fire. Terrified, I ran to the kitchen to tell my mama. Seeing the panic on my face, she went outside. The barn was indeed on fire, but not engulfed, it must've just started. The Volunteer Fire Department, my father and teenage brother Scott managed put it out before too much damage was done. I can still see Scott coming into the kitchen, his face, arms, and new white Keds sneakers blackened with soot. The next day, my mother knelt down, putting her hands on my shoulders gently, asking me how I knew the barn was burning. As I told her that a man had yelled at me, a confused look crossed her face.

The next time I heard The Voice, I was eleven. It was a woman informing me to tell my mother that she was going to be laid off from her job and needed to start looking for a new one. A few days later, it happened. One crisp Autumn afternoon when I was fourteen, my pals and I were on our daily After School Stoner Patrol, sauntering down a narrow dirt path into the woods to do shotguns of dirt weed. That day, I was last in the single file line. Carrying on and laughing as usual, The Voice, a man again, came out of nowhere, commanding "Go back *now*!". Stopping in my tracks, I yelled to the others that I had homework and had to leave. An hour later, my friends got busted by school security, complete with letters sent home to parents and indefinite detention. For some reason, even though all my friends knew I didn't ever do my homework, none of them ever assumed I was the narc.

I figured it was worth a shot at giving the phone company one last try; maybe I'd reach a nicer, more sympathetic representative. Dropping the silverware off at Disgraceland before heading up to The Boulevard to use a pay phone, I rehearsed plausible excuses along the way.

Standing in the phone booth at Hollywood and Wilcox, I pleaded with a different customer service person, trying to sound contrite, but it didn't work. Slamming the receiver onto the hook in frustration, I knew I'd fucked up big time. Hanging my head in disappointment and shame, I noticed something shiny and rectangular beneath my left motorcycle boot. At first, I thought it was a foil gum wrapper, but like the ring, which I was totally starting to regret buying, it sparkled in the sunlight. Mesmerized by the gleaming silver, I stared for a few moments before seeing the engraved dollar sign. *Holy shit, a money clip!*

Pulling the phone off the cradle again, I put it up to my ear, pretending to have a conversation. I was *really* counting the seconds in each minute out loud, I figured a half hour would be a decent amount of time for the owner of the money clip to return. As it happened, nobody else came by to use the phone, and as soon as I reached the time limit, I hung up. Grabbing the money clip from the floor, I concealed it in my hand. Crossing Wilcox, I nipped into to the lobby of The Fox Theater, heading directly to the powder room.

Pulling out the cash, my jaw dropped as I counted out $200.00 in twenties. Dashing back to the phone booth, I called a cab with my last dime. As we drove to down to the phone company, I instructed the driver to wait, something I hadn't ever done before because I *never* had enough money to take a taxi. As soon as I was finished paying, I asked the driver to take me back to Hollywood and Wilcox, where I bought a pair of kinky black spike heeled boots I'd had my eye on but never bought cause they were way too expensive. And there was still more than enough money left over to get a bottle of Jack Daniel's at Pla-Boy Liquor! Back at Disgraceland, we all swigged it directly from the bottle as I flashed my new ring, making a toast to Lady Luck.

Years later, after the internet was ubiquitous, my mind was blown when I discovered that The Voice was actually a paranormal phenomenon called *clairaudience.* Also known as clear hearing or psychic hearing, parapsychologists believe variously that clairaudient messages come from directly from Spirit, angels, or the clairaudient person's Higher Self. And I've never taken that ring off since the day The Voice told me to buy it.

IN DREAMS

For my entire life, I've had dreams that came to pass. When I was little, I thought this was the way it worked for everyone: your dreams told you what was going to happen, so that when it did, you'd know what to do. By my late teens, I realized that it wasn't the case for everyone. Any time I'd mention these oddly detailed predictive dreams to my friends, they'd give me side-eye. But when the events actually occurred, it seemed to scare them. Eventually, I just quit talking about it altogether. Even as a grown-ass woman, sometimes I'm still hesitant to discuss my psychic dreams with others, but they've always served me well, letting me know in advance the exact way a situation would unfold.

The two most significant precognitive dreams I had as an adult were absolutely *wild* in the details they revealed... as well as in the they played out in my waking life. Since the first one occurred in my early twenties and is super *juicy,* I'll whet your appetite by describing the one that helped me win a court case involving an automobile collision.

The accident had occurred around 11:00pm on Sunset Strip just west of The Roxy and The Rainbow. I'd been rear-ended at a full stop by an asshole who was texting as he rammed his black Ford Explorer SUV into the back of my gray Nissan. The impact was so extreme, I actually thought a bomb had gone off in The 9000 Building, a landmark high rise. Since the police never came to take a report and I was already in pain, I took the other driver's info so

I could get home to ice my neck. There was a lot of rear-end damage to my vehicle but it was still operable; I drove back to my place completely dazed, in shock. In a macabre synchronicity, just as I was about to turn onto my street, I witnessed an identical collision at the corner. A black Ford Explorer viciously plowed into the back of a gray Nissan... both cars were *exactly* the same models as my vehicle and the one that hit me.

By the time my case went to court a full year later, I'd been in and out of various doctor's offices and at physical therapy three times a week for months, trying to take care of the whiplash and seven bulging discs I'd sustained in the accident. I'd lost so much work from being unable to dance due to my injuries, I knew I needed to be hyper-intelligent about my looks...so I treated the court date like an acting audition. It was *imperative* that look like a Fifty-Year-Old Lady, not a hot-to-trot witchy cougar. I borrowed a conservative business suit, removed all my piercings, wore glasses in lieu of contacts, and styled my hair in a bun. A week before my deposition, I bought a pair of shoes with a medium-sized heel that would look "decent" and conservative enough for court but still be cute enough to wear for other occasions.

I had to be downtown for the deposition at 6:45 am, so I went to bed well before midnight, much earlier than the usual nocturnal hours I kept. Around 2:30 am, I woke up in a cold sweat from a dream. It was extremely vivid: the opposing attorney was trying to get me to say something that would seem to discredit all the injuries that were listed in the notes from two different doctors and my X-Ray and MRI reports. In order to prove her wrong, I slipped my high heel off and waved it in front of the video camera, so it would be on record that the soles were brand new.

Arriving at court the next morning, my lawyer met me in the lobby, waiting patiently as I sat on a bench and changed into the shoes I'd purchased for court. She reminded me to stick to the facts only, saying no more than I needed to. We entered the deposition and from the start, the lawyer from the insurance company was out for blood. She'd been grilling me for ages and it was getting exhausting.

Then, my dream played out.

"Ms. Gehman," she addressed me, cocking her head with a tight-lipped, pointedly fake smile, her gaze going directly to my feet,

"Can you *please* explain how you are wearing heels like that when you claim your spine is severely injured?"

Looking directly into her eyes, with my own identically false smile, I pulled off my right shoe with a Showbiz Flourish and held it up with the absolutely new, unblemished sole pointing straight at the camera for a l-o-n-g time.

"My injuries have prevented me from wearing anything but flip flops or Ugg Boots for the past year…" I paused dramatically for a moment before adding,

"But I since I didn't want to look disrespectful in court, I bought these shoes *only* to wear here and I changed into them in the lobby. This is the first time I've ever worn them. See? The soles are *brand new*!"

The attorney looked absolutely dumbfounded; a look of anger briefly flashed across her face. She self-corrected pretty quickly, but I caught it…and knew I'd won.

After the deposition was over, my lawyer escorted me to the lobby. Her insanely high-heeled, red-soled Louboutins clicked delightfully on the tiled floor, echoing loudly throughout the entranceway. Breaking professional protocol, she high-fived me jubilantly.

"We got this!" she said jubilantly, like a team sports player on the field after a big win.

"That shoe thing you did was brilliant! How the *hell* did you think of that? "

I shrugged before saying,

"I just stuck to the facts."

** ** **

In 1980, dialing any number on a rotary phone took a long time, but dialing a transatlantic telephone number was a huge chore. Not only where there like twelve or fifteen digits, each time you dialed one of them, the finger wheel mounted in the center of the telephone had to spring back into its initial position before you could dial the next one. Since my English boyfriend Levi Dexter was back in his home country touring with his band Levi & The Rockats, I knew the dialing pattern by heart…especially because I had a hot credit card number and often called from phone booths.

After what seemed like ages, I *finally* finished dialing and heard the welcome, tinny beeps of the British phone system ringing the number where Levi was staying.

A girl answered. Though she sounded quite sleepy, her upper crust, Sloane Ranger accent was impeccable, as were her looks, she immediately came into focus. A classic English Rose, she had periwinkle blue eyes and fair peachy skin, her naturally ginger hair fashioned a in a mod Carnaby Street 'do with long, blunt "fringe", yeah, that's Brit Speak for bangs, framing her face. Stifling a yawn, she grabbed the receiver, rubbing her eyes as she said, *Halloooeh!*

"Is Levi there?" asked.

"Do let me see," she answered quite properly.

Stretching and stifling a yawn, she asked formally,

"Whom shall I say is caaawlling?"

It was clear to me that upon hearing my American accent, she knew *exactly* who the fuck was calling. I watched her sit up in bed, swing her legs over the side and flap her feet against the wooden floor a few times to imitate what would sound like audible footsteps to someone, meaning *me,* on the other line. With that, she cuddled back up under the white duvet, rolled over and gently shook Levi awake. His clean-shaven baby face had sleep wrinkles on the left side. Calling out stridently, as though she was across the room, the girl announced performatively,

"Levi, there's a long distance call for you; it sounds like it's from the States!"

Fuckin' Limey cunt.

As he reached for the receiver, the phone rang loudly; as he spoke into the phone, it continued to ring, confusing me. I could hear him talking, greeting me affectionately, but simultaneously, I heard the insistent jangling of a ringing phone. At first, I thought there was a problem with our connection, but then I woke up...to the sound of my own phone ringing in real life!

Reaching across the kitty snoozing on my pillow, I grabbed the receiver off the cradle and heard Levi's voice. He'd interrupted a dream that was so realistic, it was as though I was in the room with him and the redhead. Instantly, I became suspicious.

"Where are you?" I asked as casually as possible.

It wasn't an odd question, because neither of us had enough money to call each other unless it was on a hot credit card, or a "borrowed" phone, which usually meant crashing a party at some rich person's house and locking yourself in the bedroom to make a clandestine long distance call.

Levi said he was in London at Virgin Records headquarters. He was sitting at the receptionist's desk, using the free international line to call me while his manager, the legendary Leee Black Childers, was in an A&R meeting, trying to get The Rockats a deal.

The moment Levi told me, I envisioned that same girl and it became abundantly clear that she was the receptionist. This time, she was dolled up for her Cool Record Company Job in retro Twiggy-style baby blue eyeshadow carefully selected to match her vintage 1960s Portobello Road puffy-sleeved baby doll dress exactly. To my credit, I played it cool, but how could I not? I mean, who the hell busts their boyfriend for cheating…on a transatlantic phone call because of a dream? Luckily, I've always been tactful, so I decided it was prudent to wait until Levi got home before addressing his-*thanks Hank Williams*-cheatin' heart.

A few weeks later, the band arrived a jetlagged mess at my punk house Disgraceland, where Levi had been living with me. The plan was to decompress and play a few local gigs before going on a cross country US tour. As we sat around the living room drinking Lucky Lager and playing obscure rockabilly 45's, the guys talked about the band's meetings at various record companies and the gigs they'd played at Dingwall's in London.

I decided now was as good a time as any to bring up the subject of the Limey Cunt.

"So how'd Virgin go?' I asked all innocently,

"Didn't you call me from a receptionist's desk there?'

Levi nodded affirmatively... *before* I described what the chick looked like and the outfit she had on as well as the fact that the phone on her desk was red. At that point, their manager Leee's face drained of color and Levi cocked his head, a strange look on his face. The other band members looked confounded.

Absolutely unedited words tumbled from my mouth quickly, but they were stated calmly as facts, rather than the product of-*thanks Elvis*-a suspicious mind.

"I know you slept with her the night before you were at her desk calling me."

As I launched into the part about the cream-colored duvet in the dream and the chick's accent, the glances exchanged among the guys were now nervous and more than a little concerned. I related watching the girl pretend she was getting out of bed and her footsteps…all of it.

Everyone in the room was silent except for me. Levi looked absolutely gob-smacked; Leee shook his head, his eyebrows raised a quizzically; maybe even a tad expectantly.

Finally, the drummer shooed the elephant from the room by asking a question that went right along with the theme, but managed to deftly to change the subject:

"So…do you think our touring vehicle is safe?

I asked if it was a white station wagon; he said yes.

"It's fine," I answered.

Levi and I never discussed the girl again, and the battered old station wagon went above and beyond the call of duty, serving the band well for the whole tour.

SPIRIT COMMUNICATION A GO-GO

From 1978 to 1988, I lived at Disgraceland, the most notorious punk crash pad in Hollywood. Disgraceland was a Who's Who of the international punk scene. Almost every band you could think from that time period stopped by to party, often staying for *days*. Most of them were close friends in newly formed bands; several went on to become rock'n'roll legends. To name just a few: The Red Hot Chili Peppers, Billy Idol, Social Distortion, The Vandals, Stiv Bators, TSOL, The Replacements, Madness, and Guns N' Roses. Some of our guests were already famous; living legends such as Screamin' Jay Hawkins, Jayne County, Angela Bowie and my longtime pal Joan Jett.

Originally, I moved into Disgraceland with Kid Congo Powers who was in The Gun Club, and our friend Marci Blaustein, who wound up working with Lydia Lunch. Over the years, the housemates changed constantly. My most consistent roomies were also my longest running besties: writer and Lame Flames singer Iris Berry and Belinda Carlisle of The Go-Go's.

When Belinda first moved in, The Go-Go's had already played quite a few shows and were opening for more established bands, but were still pretty much unknown outside of Los Angeles and the United Kingdom. While Belinda was living at Disgraceland, the band got signed to IRS Records, but by the time she moved out in 1982, it was less about having her own place than it was an absolute necessity. The Go-Go's first album *Beauty And The Beat* had rocketed up the charts to Number One and in an instant, Disgraceland turned into a new wave version of The Beatles' film *A Hard Day's Night*.

Kids from the nearby schools somehow discovered Belinda lived there, storming our pad nonstop, pressing their faces up against the windows hoping to catch a glimpse of her. Huddling on our front porch, they'd patiently wait for hours, hoping for an autograph.

From the moment Belinda and I met in 1976, at The Beverly Hilton, waiting for Queen and hoping Freddie Mercury would stroll through the lobby, we clicked like long lost soul sisters. Both of us identified as groupies; we were wild, fun loving rock'n'roll chicks. Fascinated with Old Hollywood, we aspired to the Tinsel Town Glamour of that bygone era, dressing like punkified 1940s starlets. Once she moved into Disgraceland, we discovered that we had something else in common: an obsession with all things occult.

The Panpipes, which was the oldest and most famous witchy shop in Los Angeles, was directly around the corner from our house. We'd spend hours in there getting custom spell candles made, flipping through witchcraft books, buying Tarot cards, incense and charms. We had altars in our rooms and started saving our menstrual blood in little glass phials to use for sex magick, hoping to lure the boys we had crushes on into our tangled web of desire.

Habitually going out to clubs every night, Belinda and I would get get riotously drunk before stopping at The Rainbow parking lot to check out the scene and buy Quaaludes, which we promptly ingested. Because of our penchant for nightlife, our days usually started in the early afternoon. We'd hang out in our undies on the couch wondering what the hell had happened to our house keys or purses, filling in each other's blanks on the events of the previous night.

Drinking Tab to chase our hangovers, we'd both finally get dressed, watching old black and white movies on the television that'd come from the trash…or playing with the Ouija Board I'd had since I was twelve. Since our area of central Hollywood was so haunted, we'd often try to connect with the spirits of the starlets and contract players we saw in those films.

During our most memorable session, the planchette whizzed around the board like a carnival ride, before finally spelling out:

HOUSE DIRTY

We caught each other's eyes in amazement before taking an objective look at our living room. As usual, the floor around my janky Sears Roebuck stereo was strewn with records and singles, mostly out of their jackets. Empty beer cans and overflowing ashtrays obliterated the surface of the coffee table; the mantlepiece of the non-functional fireplace was decorated with a bust of Elvis in Alice Cooper makeup, surrounded by empty fifths of booze. There were vintage Frederick's of Hollywood spike-heel mules, piles of petticoats, fishnet stockings, 1950s bullet-cupped brassieres, assorted leather jackets and ratty vintage dresses entirely covering the couch and end tables.

At that point, we both realized that the message spelled out on the board was *definitely* proof there were spirits around us.

"That's pretty fuckin' rude!" Belinda said indignantly as I simultaneously yelled,

"Fuck you!"

Though our fingertips were still lightly parked on the planchette, it immediately started moving swiftly again on its own. This time, it spelled:

S H U T U P SLUTS

I felt a cold chill up my spine and Belinda inhaled sharply; it spooked the hell out of us. Exchanging glances of genuine horror, we got up in unison, promptly put the board away and didn't touch it again for ages.

BAD JUJU

In 1980, my friend Anna Statman and I made a pact to take a train across America to visit the cities our favorite music came from. We worked multiple jobs around the clock for months in order to finance the trip. In addition to an awful stint clerking at the hosiery counter of *The Broadway* department store, I wrote feature stories and my rock'n'roll gossip column *L.A. De Da* for *LA Weekly*. Anna and I also worked together as film editors at The Nuart Theatre, cutting out deteriorated sequences of the old celluloid films that came in for showing. The attic with the editing bays was stuffy and the hours were l-o-n-g. But the job was fun as we repaired classic Midnight Movies like *Reefer Madness*, *Pink Flamingos*, *Night Of The Living Dead*, and of course, *The Rocky Horror Picture Show*.

After months of this, we'd saved enough to book our tickets on The Sunset Limited, the southernmost cross-country Amtrak route. Both of us were super excited.

Just before we left, The Cramps played The Whisky A Go to support their first record, *Songs The Lord Taught Us*. That night, as a joke to celebrate their single *Garbage Man*, the record company gave the band an aluminum trashcan full of "bum wine": Thunderbird, MD 2020 and the appropriately-named Night Train. Since it was such foul swill, none of the usual dressing room freeloaders drank it, so as opposed to letting it go to waste, Anna and I decided to take it all home to bring along on the train as refreshments.

Bill "Buster" Bateman, drummer of rootsy band The Blasters helped us load the heavy, clanking Hefty Bag into Anna's car. Buster was handsome in a rugged in an old school hoodlum way and tons of fun. Since my boyfriend was on tour overseas, were having a little fling together. During our goodbyes, I said I'd miss him. Giving me a little kiss and squeeze, he asked me to check in with him by calling collect once or twice a week. He also told me to stay out of trouble…but he already knew me well enough to know that I probably wouldn't.

The train was a blast. Since Anna and I could only afford coach, we made new friends by handing out wine bottles like Halloween candy. We met servicemen on leave, cute old ladies in dainty travelling hats, wizened old farmers in overalls and plaid shirts and hippie backpackers. Chugging along through the vast Texas desert, we'd hit the Bar Car, where everyone was shitfaced, telling jokes, smoking cigars, and playing cards. A foxy young Creole conductor even slid us into an empty *roomette* in the Sleeper Car on the second night cause we'd given him a few bottles of Night Train.

Memphis included pilgrimages to Graceland, Sun Studios, Beale Street and hanging out with Tav Falco's band The Panther Burns, with whom The Cramps had hooked us up. At the time, pop legend Alex Chilton of The Box Tops and Big Star was playing with them. Anna and I go-go danced on stage with The Panther Burns the night they played at a venue called The Well. In the middle of their set, the cops raided the club, ostensibly looking for underage drinkers. Alex dragged me offstage, hustling me into a broom closet, where to my complete disbelief, he promptly lit a joint. Who *does* that in the middle of a bust? A few seconds later, an officer flung the door open and as he did, Alex seized me, pretending we were kissing; the poor cop got so flustered he mumbled "Excuse me" …and shut the door!

An after party and a fist fight later, we were on our way to New York City. Though Anna and I were hung over on arrival, that didn't stop us from spending every night at CBGB, Max's Kansas City, The Mudd Club and Danceteria. On our last night in town we went to Hurrah, where for some unknown reason, Thin Lizzy's guitarist Phil Lynott let us, and all the friends we had in tow, drink on his tab all night long, without even trying to take either one of us home.

Our first stop in New Orleans was by far the wildest. Setting the tone for the entire trip, we went out on the town every damn night. We stayed with my friend Andie and her affable, hilarious husband Joseph. Andie and I had never met in person before, but we'd been pen-pals for years, writing novel-length letters to each other, usually about the music we liked. I'd send her glittery T-Rex shirts I'd made by hand; she'd send me shoeboxes full of Mardi Gras beads, which in those days, were made of glass. Because she'd been born and raised in New Orleans, she knew practically everyone in town and had the 411 on the hotspots that only the locals knew about. We'd hit up a series of bars in the French Quarter before going to see bands play and winding up at their after parties each night.

Anna and I were impressed; New Orleans was way cooler than we'd hoped it would be, as were the people. Everyone was so nice...and quirky. The moment we stepped off the train, we spotted an intriguing guy who looked like the love child of Little Richard and Voodoo queen Marie Laveau. With a pencil thin mustache and hair in curlers tied up in a shiny red do-rag, he sported a frilly shirt woman's and wicked black cat-eye sunglasses. Fantastic music was everywhere, pouring out of speakers or live the in clubs and backyard parties: Swamp Blues, Delta Blues, Dixieland, Zydeco and old school Rockabilly. Raucous impromptu Second Line parades popped up on every corner, following brass bands playing for weddings or birthdays.

The centuries-old cobblestone streets, Creole architecture and the wondrously spooky graveyards charmed us to no end. The proliferation of Voodoo and Hoodoo in the city was incredible; magic was really woven into the fabric of everyday life. When I laughed at a Voodoo *veve* spray painted on the side of a garbage bin, Joseph informed me that it wasn't graffiti. He told me was painted on the trash can as warning; if anyone tried to steal the trash can, they'd face serious consequences.

One morning, Anna and I wanted to walk the levees, so Andrea dropped us off before going to work. Mesmerized by the sheer power of the Mississippi, the opaque chocolate brown water also had a unique sound. With each ebb and flow, it tinkled loudly because of the incredible amount of glass it contained. We watched for ages as newer bottles shattered on the rocks and the older, water-dulled shards of amber, red and blue glass swirled like clothes in a washing machine.

Walking under the under the massive Live Oaks along the levee, we admired the long layers of lacey gray Spanish Moss hanging from the trees like a bayou fantasy come to life. It was really picturesque in a spooky Southern Gothic way. Our budget was so limited, I wanted to pick some, figuring it would make a terrific, *and free*, New Orleans souvenir. I tried for ages to get some but was too short to reach it; no matter how many times I jumped, arms flailing wildly, I couldn't grab any of the gray gossamer strands. In desperation, I flagged down a tall passerby.

"What y'all want with t*hat*?" he asked, eyeing me dubiously.

I didn't know it at the time, but Spanish Moss (sometimes known colloquially as "Devil's Beard") has long been associated with

Voodoo and Hoodoo, the Southern folk magic also called Root Work or Conjure. It can be used as an ingredient in Mojo Bags to draw money as well as for spells that involve either love or revenge. In sympathetic magic, it's reputed be an extremely potent ingredient, used for either purpose. Most commonly, it's stuffed inside a doll baby or Voodoo doll along with personal concerns like hair, fingernail clippings or even a cigarette butt that touched the target's lips.

All it took was a little cajoling, plus what a couple of locals had been calling my "sexy Yankee accent", to convince the guy to help me. Boosting me up onto one shoulder, he was patient as I snatched wildly at the lacy tendrils. Even as twigs, leaves, dirt, dust, mold spores and a plethora of dead spiders and other insects rained onto his head, he retained his Southern Gentleman charm. Thanking him while stuffing the Spanish *Mess* into my purse, Anna and I explored Audabon Park before heading back to Andie's.

Dumping the Spanish Moss on the kitchen counter, I sorted through it, cleaning out all the detritus, separating it into big piles. Addressing an envelope to Buster, I scooped up a healthy amount, packing it tightly inside along with a little note I'd kissed with freshly-applied lipstick. I ran out to the corner mailbox and the humidity was so high that by the time I got back I was drenched in sweat and needed a Disco Nap. I was startled awake by the sound of yelling in the kitchen.

"Son of a bitch! What the hell is all this?", Joseph bellowed.

Feeling like a really bad guest for leaving the moss scattered over the clean kitchen counter, I answered contritely,

"Oh, I'm so sorry, I didn't mean to make such a mess!"

"What's it even *doing* here?," he hollered back. He was irate, beside himself, shaking with rage.

He'd seemed so sweet the whole time; I'd never seen this side of him. Wondering if he had anger issues, I quickly started sweeping up the large piles with my hands, only succeeding in spreading it around further, dropping large, snaky tendrils onto the clean white floor.

"GET THIS SHIT OUTTA HERE RIGHT NOW!", Joseph roared,

"IT'S BAD JUJU!"

Realizing that I thought he was mad about the mess I'd left, Joseph regained his composure and apologized. Then, with a concerned look on his face, he explained that Spanish Moss was not only unlucky, but something to be feared. He detailed all the awful things that could happen to someone who was cursed with Spanish Moss. Clearly, he took everything he was saying extremely seriously and believed in magic. Fascinated with the culture of New Orleans, I hung on every word he said.

Anna and I had been in Memphis for a couple of days before I realized that I'd fucked up bigtime: I'd completely forgotten to tell Buster about the Spanish Moss. The operator put the collect call through, and he picked up on the first ring.

"Boy, am I glad to hear from *you*," he said happily,

"You're the best thing that's happened to me all week!"

He asked if I was having fun; I assured him I was. But before I had a chance to tell him why I was calling, he launched into a tale straight out of a supernatural thriller. He said he'd checked his mailbox a few days ago and was stoked to see a letter from me.

Ripping it open, he was confused at the fauna exploding from the envelope, but eager to read the note inside. Hurrying up the cement stairs to his porch, he missed a step and tripped, breaking his ankle.

After spending all afternoon in the emergency room, he somehow managed to play the Blasters' gig that night at The Starwood. Using the foot without the cast on it to operate the kick drum pedals, he played just fine...for a few songs. Then, in a freak accident onstage, he sliced his entire hand open on a crash cymbal. Performance adrenalin prevented him from feeling the deep gash, and he continued playing the song until it finished. The blood spurting from the wound splashed all over the entire drum kit so spectacularly that evidently, several audience members thought it was a special effect and started applauding wildly. The rest of the band realized what was going on, aborting the set on the spot to take Buster to his second Emergency Room Visit in less than twelve hours. It took several stitches to fix him up and the doctor said he'd be out of commission for a few weeks.

I felt absolutely awful, overcome with guilt. *If only I'd called him sooner!* I wracked my brains trying to think of something to comfort him from across the country, but before I thought of anything particularly soothing some I blurted,

"Hey! You know that Spanish Moss that was in the letter? I was calling you to tell you to throw it away!"

I didn't even give him a chance to answer.

"Get that shit outta your house right now!", I shrieked,

"It's *bad juju!*"

ESCAPE FROM HOUDINI MOUNTAIN

It was 1981 and I'd been slam dancing the night away at the legendary club The Starwood in West Hollywood, with my pals Kid Congo of The Gun Club, artist Brad Dunning, and a noted cult rock star, who will hence be dubbed Mr. Monster. I had a little crush on Mr. Monster... but then, *everybody* did. He was tall and rangy, good-looking in a macabre way, like Elvis From Hell. He was infamous for being completely wild, both on and off stage: climbing on top of amps in stiletto heels with a mic shoved into his mouth, or swinging Tarzan style from catwalks and balconies, dangling precariously over the audience. So when somebody suggested we all drop acid, I didn't hesitate. Last Call rolled around a little too soon, and we beat it out of the club before the lights went up.

After killing a fifth of Jack Daniel's and beaucoup Budweiser at Disgraceland, the punk house I shared with Kid, we were all itching to get into trouble. Brad suggested we go to the old Harry Houdini mansion, up in the wilds of Laurel Canyon. The next thing I clearly remember is all of us running through the underbrush, screaming "HARRY! HAAAAAAA-REEEEEEE!" like Allison Hayes as *The Fifty Foot Woman* when she got stuck in those pesky high-tension wires, yelling for her husband. We joked about Houdini's ghost acknowledging us, because apparently, when he'd been alive, he was really into séances.

Mr. Monster and I both heard music coming from Houdini's guest house, rock and roll. For some reason, even though it was blasting so loud it was echoing through the entire canyon, Kid and Brad insisted that we were hallucinating, so Mr. Monster and I split off to investigate. By this time, we were all full on tripping; that kind of heart-skipping, strobing, blood-and-rust-in-your-mouth, peaking LSD high.

Brad and Kid made their way down the hillside and back onto the street to the car, thinking we'd only be a minute. Mr. Monster and I trudged through the woods following the music, which seemed to be coming from the Houdini guest house. The entire estate, built in 1918, was magnificent; there were terraced gardens and a deep-water tank where Houdini practiced his legendary feats of escape. There were several caves on the property, too: some natural, others man-made. Apparently, there was also an elevator that carried guests to a hidden tunnel built beneath Laurel Canyon, which lead to the other side of the street where the guest house was located. It had been built into the side of the hill, with windows about a story and a half up from the ground.

Mr. Monster, who in his stocking feet was tall enough to give any NBA star a run for his money, suggested that if I stood on his shoulders and then he stood up, I'd be able to spy into one of the windows. Loaded and devil-may-care enough to actually think this was a good idea in the complete darkness on a rocky, uneven hillside, I climbed aboard his shoulders. I held onto his upraised arms as he stood up shakily. Steadying myself with one hand clutching the rotting window ledge, I peered inside the guest house.

For a split second, I thought I was already hallucinating. There were about ten bikers: really big, scary, Bachman Turner Overdrive-sized bikers, with beards, beer bellies and straggly hair, all wearing greasy denim and black leather jackets. They were sitting around this trashed room with dripping candles everywhere, listening to a boom box, drinking beer and smoking some very skunky weed. Back then, punks were punks, bikers were bikers, there was absolutely no crossover whatsoever. At that point in time, movie star and motorcycle enthusiast Mickey Rourke probably hadn't even entertained the idea of riding a Harley.

All of a sudden, one of the bikers happened to look up, spotting me with a huge, cartoon-like double take. Evidently, he thought I was hanging on the side of the house ... and couldn't believe his good fortune at discovering a nubile teenage girl clinging to his window ledge at, like, 4:00am!

"No, it's okay," I said, casually, as though all this was *normal,*

"I'm standing on someone."

"Well, why don't you both come in?" the biker said hospitably, gesturing to a side path that led to the door.

I jumped off Mr. Monster 's shoulders and we walked up to the house. We were immediately offered refreshments, contraband, and a guided tour of the residence, where the whole gang was apparently *homesteading.* It was ridiculously unbelievable, making any Roger Corman chopper-trash B movie look positively tame in comparison.

So, we're sitting in the bathroom, Mr. Monster and me, on the crumbling old porcelain claw-footed tub, with the Leader Of The Pack, who is astride the toilet. He's a skinny, pale guy with darting Crystal-Meth-Powered eyes and a Mansonesque intensity. We're smoking a joint. There's a stoned-out lull in the conversation, and The Leader gets all weird and silent. Abruptly, with what can only be described as a sinisterly quiet psychotic rage, he says,

"I was in 'Nam, you know. One day I got this letter that my stepmother, *the fuckin' bitch*, slit her own throat with a milk bottle!"

Mr. Monster and I share a brief sidelong glance, and in my acid consciousness, I knew I wasn't the only one who was starting to get scared. Then The Leader said, with all the veins in his neck and forehead bulging,

"When I found out she did that, man… *it made the war for me!*"

He busted into a red-faced, clenched-jawed, sociopathic grin.

I squeezed Mr. Monster's hand in what I hoped was a signal; he made some off-the-cuff excuse about leaving, but The Leader wouldn't hear of it. Not wanting to offend him since it was clearly apparent, he was deranged, we agreed to go and look at his pride and joy, his Master Bedroom. The Leader led us out into the woods behind the guest house, further up the hill. His bedroom turned out to be under a flagstone gazebo that was fitted with a lighting fixture that had a bare bulb in it, which actually worked. The Leader pulled the switch, and sitting on top of a massive pile of trash was a round, king-sized bed with a ratty velveteen leopard print bedspread. Astonished, Mr. Monster and I stared at the scene in silence until The Leader motioned us back to the guest house. In a hushed, confidential tone, he leaned in close, saying we could use the bed if we wanted to "make it", licking his lips lewdly for emphasis.

What we did make was more excuses for leaving *right now*, but we didn't want to appear as though we were freaking out…and our mutual anxiety at the situation was growing exponentially with each second.

As The Leader took off to get us a new beer, Mr. Monster glanced at me quickly, grabbed my hand and we made a run for it. Seemingly out of nowhere, like a character in a cheap Ninja film, the leader jumped into the middle of the path in front of us, demanding to know where the fuck we thought we were going. He herded us back to the house, and after another failed escape attempt, I blurted out to The Leader that we'd decided after all we'd like to stay so we could "make it." I think I even winked.

Mr. Monster and I trudged back up the slope to the gazebo, sitting on the bed in the dark feeling all paranoid… like... maybe if we waited there long enough, the bikers would simply forget about us. We were there for maybe five minutes, maybe twenty or thirty, *who knows?*

Simultaneously, we both started making fake sex sounds, moaning, groaning and bouncing on the bed, to fool the bikers into thinking we were fucking. Mr. Monster pulled his at his cheeks, making loud, salacious slurping noises. Somehow, I'm not sure exactly how, we really started having sex. As we made out furiously, Mr. Monster yanked off my tattered jeans and white '50s majorette boots in one fell swoop.

I clearly remember lying beneath him in my little 1950s angora sweater, laughing hysterically, staring at my feet on his shoulders in the moonlight in their shocking pink, fuzzy Gorilla Sox (with a separate sleeve for each toe) and thinking how completely insane this entire thing was. Here we were, tripping our brains out in the middle of Laurel Canyon, abandoned by our friends, held hostage by a biker gang, and now we were fucking! It was like a drug-laced punk rock version of *The Rocky Horror Show*: maniacs, a castle, and kinky sex on a round, king sized bed sitting atop a pile of trash in a dark forest.

Suddenly, in muted tones and then getting increasingly louder, we heard singing. At first, we assumed it was coming from the boom box, but because the underbrush was rustling suspiciously and there was muffled laughter, we realized it was the bikers. Hidden somewhere in the shadowy brush on the hill, they serenaded us, singing in *a cappella*, like a professional choir in perfect harmony:

"In the jungle, the mighty jungle, the lion sleeps tonight..." complete with the "Ow-wee-mo-weh, ow-wee-mo-weh" choruses.

Naturally, this took things to another dimension, with or without the acid. Mr. Monster and I started laughing hysterically. I thought: *If we're gonna die, this is the best way to go ever!*

Mr. Monster and I were both so wasted, I'm not even sure if we came. In telepathic unison, we jumped off the bed, got our clothes together, and careened down the hill through the trees and bushes. Breathless and covered in sticks and twigs, we hitched a ride down to Sunset Boulevard with an old man who was delivering the morning paper. Sitting in the cargo deck of his vintage pick-up truck, we watched the sun rise over Hollywood.

The next afternoon, Mr. Monster came by to bring me his newly released British import 45, appropriately titled *Love Me*.

That afternoon, when I finally called Brad to tell him what happened, he listened in amazement, confirming that Kid and he had waited over three hours for us on the street before going home.

Exactly a week later, reading the *LA Times*, I saw a cryptic report in the Metro Section. It stated that two teenagers who'd been trespassing one night up near the Houdini Mansion had been shot with a BB gun by "transients." No suspects had been taken into custody.

THE ACE OF SPADES AND THE HIGH PRIESTESS

My twin sisters couldn't stop carrying on about the psychic they'd just been to; they said he was so spot on it was *batshit*. They didn't lean towards the occult the way I did, but both of them ran with a Hollywood crowd who were all in The Industry, and at the time, anything even remotely New Age was all the rage. Basically, Hollywood was the same as high school: once an A-lister discovered a new trend, whether it was a restaurant, interior decorator, vacation spot or Yoga instructor, it became Flavor Of The Moment.

In 1997, it was super hip to join J-Date, a Beverly Hills-based matchmaking service that practically hooked up the entire Entertainment Biz in a matter of months. When that got old, it became absolutely *de riguer* to get a reading from psychic Jim Diehl; he was the spiritual advisor to the stars, everyone who was anyone wouldn't think of signing a deal before consulting with him.

The twins had always been skeptical when it came to anything even slightly woo-woo, but they both sang his praises non-stop. Each of them made appointments with him, *under fake names,* ostensibly to test his intuitive powers, hoping they could call him out somehow. One returned from her reading with such glowing reviews that the other booked an appointment right away. She snuck in to get a reading the afternoon her husband was taking the

California Bar exam. She was flabbergasted when Jim Diehl opened the door, greeting her with,

"Your husband's going to make a great lawyer!"

I was so insanely jealous of their readings, my sister Eddie booked one for me as a birthday present, letting me know what to expect in minute detail.

"Don't say anything to him, just let him talk. Everything he told me was spot on, it was *psychotic*! He has an open Bible on his desk, and he keeps his hand on it the whole time. He shuffled up a deck of playing cards and pulled one out for me, he'll probably do that for you too."

I'd been obsessed with the occult and experiencing paranormal phenomena my entire life, but until Eddie hooked me up with Jim Diehl, I'd never had a session with a legitimate psychic. My only experiences were with Storefront Psychics. Many are charlatans, throwing down a few cards or performing a cursory egg cleansing to absorb negative energy from the body. Then, feigning horror, they'll swear there's a curse on you that *only* they can remove… for hundreds of dollars. Well aware of all this, I was nevertheless fascinated, drawn to them because of the whole Fortuneteller Mystique, a carnie-adjacent aesthetic I absolutely *adored*.

In the late 1980s I paid a visit to Mrs. Lee, who'd been set up for years a few blocks down the street from me in a sprawling two-story Craftsman home. There were security bars on the windows covered by banners printed with hearts, roses, the seven chakras and angels. Two big-ass white plaster lions guarded the porch like a Vegas version of The New York Public Library. It was such a spectacular example of my beloved Fortuneteller Mystique that for ages, I'd been curious not only about getting my own fortune told, but what the inside of her house looked like. And hey, if she told me I was cursed, I'd just consider it a bonus, well worth the ten bucks.

The interior, and Mrs. Lee herself, were everything I'd fantasized about and more; I was in Fortuneteller Heaven. A teenage kid dressed as a maid answered the door and Mrs. Lee swept down the stairs in a pink house dress with a floral scarf wrapped around her head; she was loaded down with jangly gold jewelry. There were ornately framed paintings of Jesus swathed in pastel robes and baroque sofas with tuck'n'roll upholstery covered in clear plastic. Mrs. Lee read my palm with my arm stretched out on the glass top of an antique Chinese table that had intricate three-dimensional carvings. I could barely focus on what she was saying as I marveled over the detailed microscopic mountains, forests, villages, people and animals. According to her, I was going to have a long life and would "know some troubles", but I'd also have many loves. To my dismay, she didn't mention anything about a curse. Undoubtedly, she realized I didn't have the kind of dough it took to have a curse removed the second I walked in.

The next reader I visited was on The Santa Monica Pier, with the sound of the waves and music from the carousel in the background. She was set up in a dingy shop that had a buzzing neon PSYCHIC sign and a dusty phrenology head in the window; the oriental carpets were covered with footprints made of damp beach sand. I could feel the woman's eyes assessing me shrewdly as soon I entered, taking in my faded ripped Levi's, black leather jacket and scuffed cowboy boots. Pulling out a chair at the purple velvet-draped table, she motioned me to sit. She was in the middle of shuffling the cards and hadn't even laid them down as she stated soulfully,

"You never felt really, truly loved…is that right, baby?"

I was about to answer but she didn't give me a chance, continuing,

"You were very rebellious as a child!"

"What makes you say *that*?", I asked, all faux innocent, seconds before blowing my cover, and the entire reading, by exploding into uproarious laugher.

So while I was thrilled by Eddie's description of her session with Jim Diehl, I was still a little gun shy: after the other two readings, I had no idea what to expect. Maybe Eddie had applied generalized statements as information pertinent to her own situation?

The night before my appointment, I was giddy with expectation. As I brushed my teeth before bed, I thought of Eddie saying Jim Diehl had pulled a playing card; simultaneously, an image of the Ace Of Spades popped into my head. *Would that be my card?* Staring into the mirror with a mouthful of toothpaste, I said out loud to my reflection:

What makes you think you'll get The Ace Of Spades? Is it cause you love Motorhead?

Speaking of rock'n'roll, oddly enough, Jim Diehl lived a couple of doors down from Joan Jett's old apartment, which was directly across the street from The Whisky A Go-Go. I'd spent several nights a week in the late 1970s at Joan's partying both before and after seeing bands play at The Whisky. I saw this as a good omen.

He greeted me with a friendly smile and kind but piercing, arctic blue eyes. Over his shoulder, I noticed, shades of Mrs. Lee, the couch was covered in clear plastic. He had a couple of adorable lap dogs, the Yorkie had a top-knot tied with a baby blue satin bow, and the coffee table was strewn with the latest tabloids. Ushering me into the reading room, he sat at the desk, opening a large, well worn Bible. Placing his hand upon one of the pages, he started talking quickly.

"If you get the opportunity to take a trip to Hawaii in the very near future, you should go! I also see you travelling to Europe soon. There are palm-trees there...but I am not sure *why*. It's definitely Europe, though. I'm getting the name Tim, as in T-I-M; this will be significant during that trip."

He paused, taking a quick sip of water before continuing,

"You should really change your name; you need to adopt a symbol of royalty as part of it...I know this sounds *really* corny, very cliché, but I see you in ancient Egypt as some kind of royalty, and when you make this name change with the royal title, you'll have a lot of success in your career."

None of it made sense to me...like, at all. Also: *What the fuck with the palm trees?* I had zero intention of changing my name; I was already having success as a writer. I'd been freelancing for every major rock'n'roll publication for years, since I was a teenager. I was a staff writer for a couple of weekly papers and a monthly magazine in Los Angeles, plus my first two books had already been released to critical acclaim. There was no way in hell I was gonna to start using a pen name at this stage of the game; what would be the point?

He went on to tell me I'd get a part on a major television show, but in an unusual way and that I'd also make a lot of money from it...which I severely doubted. As I tried to keep a composed, neutral look on my face, he got out a deck of playing cards. He shuffled a few times before placing them face-down on the table. Running his fingertip along the stack vertically, he looked me directly in the eyes as he asked,

"You know you're incredibly psychic, right?"

Then he pulled my card.

"Ace Of Spades!" he announced, holding the card right in front of my face as my jaw hit the floor in astonishment.

"The High Priestess; The Oracle... you *need* to develop your gift! You should be speaking, writing, teaching. All of it! You'll be very good at what you do, and you'll be helping people. You'll be able to make them see and understand and do things that they normally wouldn't be able to."

Even though the first part of our session seemed nonsensical, and the teaching stuff didn't ring any bells, the crazy synchronicity of the Ace Of Spades shattered my mind to bits...it was far, far better than being told I needed to have a curse removed!

The day after the reading, my friend Valarie called, asking if I wanted to go to Hawaii with her... in three days, at the end of the week. Her boyfriend had been in Honolulu for months working on the new *Godzilla* film and missed her. Since he spent long hours working, he said it would be great if she brought a friend along for daytime companionship. I said yes without even thinking about it.

Score one point for Jim Diehl!

In 1998, several more things that Jim Diehl had predicted occurred.

One night while working at my regular belly dance gig, a waiter came into the dressing room saying I had a caller waiting on the restaurant's phone. It was after 10:00pm, and I never got calls on that phone, so I hoped it wasn't an emergency. It turned out to be a casting director for the sitcom *The Nanny*, asking me if I could make an audition for the show at 7:00am the next morning; they needed belly dancers. I accepted, and along with three other dancers, got the part. The circumstances were unusual, and the pay was great: a substantial base fee, and to this day I still get residuals from Season Five, Episode 14, *Not Without My Nanny,* which first aired January 28, 1998

Score two points for Jim Diehl!

Shortly after that, I got another call that elucidated the whole "palm trees in Europe" puzzle. My director friend Steve Balderson's first film *Pep Squad* had been accepted into the 51st Cannes Film Festival. It was scheduled for screening and Steve would be speaking on a panel ...smack dab on the *palm-lined* Croisette on the French Riviera. I had a song on the soundtrack but hadn't acted in *Pep Squad.* Steve wanted me along as an attention-getter; figuring with my flashy looks and outgoing nature, we'd make a lot of connections. The moment I knew I was going to France, I contacted my arty, years-younger Swiss lover Daniel. We'd been apart for months and arranged to meet in Paris for a tryst before I went to Cannes. I called a travel agent who arranged the flights and booked me into an affordable hotel in the quaint, charming Montmartre district of Paris. When I received the hardcopy ticket and hotel reservation, I was dumbfounded that the place I'd be staying in was called Timhotel Montmartre. *TIM, what the actual? Score three points for Jim Deihl!*

That wasn't the only synchronicity. The night before I left, Eddie and I were at a Rite Aid at midnight buying travel-sized items when we spotted a guy with his arm stuck into the free blood pressure checking machine. Sweaty and twitchy, he had on aviator shades at midnight. I knew a tweaker when I saw one.

"Holy crap! That looks like Jean-Claude van Damme!" Eddie exclaimed, hiding in the vitamin aisle, trying to get a better look.

Just then, the store's loudspeaker blared,

"Will the owner of the silver Mercedes with its lights on parked sideways across the handicapped space please move their car?"

Throwing away all pretense of espionage, Eddie shrieked,

"Silver *Mercedes*? It's *gotta* be him!"

Simultaneously, Van Damme (or cough-cough the alleged *doppleganger*) yanked his arm out of the blood pressure machine, sprinting towards the parking lot entrance.

On the way to the airport the next day, I joked about meeting The Muscles From Brussels in Cannes, telling him we both had something in common: late nights at the Hollywood Rite Aid.

The stop in Paris to see Daniel turned out to be significant, alright, and not just because it took place at Timhotel. It was three days of lovin' and fun, but on the last day, we had a such a spectacular breakup, I cried through the entire plane trip down to the French Riviera. Determined to put Paris behind me, I got all gussied up, aiming to go out on the town and get into some serious Movie Biz trouble. I was definitely having visons of piles of cocaine with buckets of Cristal as a chaser.

Arriving in the Carlton Hotel lobby, I looked like a million bucks. Waiting to meet Steve, a guy wearing an all-access press badge struck up a conversation. After some small talk, he invited me to a penthouse soiree that evening. I wanted to keep my options open for my first night on the loose in the French Riviera, so I flirtatiously asked who was hosting the event. When the reporter said it was for Jean-Claude Van Damme, I accepted the invitation without a second thought.

And just to put the synchronicity way over the top, I had no idea what the festival's closing film was going to be until I was already in Cannes. Turned out it was *Godzilla*, which was the sole reason I'd gone to Hawaii.

Score four points for Jim Diehl!

After so much of what he said in my first session came to pass, I booked others and they were always incredible.

It wasn't until almost a decade later that I realized almost everything else he'd predicted had also come true. At the time, I was hardly ever home, busy travelling all over the world to teach and perform belly dance. When I finally got a break in my schedule, I decided I needed to get my house in order since I was going to be in LA for a while. I opened up a dust-covered box in the back of my closet and it was full of cassettes. Most were from interviews I'd done, but one wasn't labelled. Popping the tape into my boombox, it turned out to be the first reading I'd gotten from Jim Diehl.

I got chills when I heard the part about "adopting a symbol of royalty". Making my dance website the early 2000s, I searched domain names and found out that Farhana.com was already in use…by a plastic surgery clinic in Jalalabad, Pakistan. My stage name Farhana was a loose translation of my real name, Pleasant, meaning "happy or pleasant

girl" so I was pretty pissed I couldn't use Farhana because it was already taken. I decided instead to use the nickname bestowed upon me by other dancers because my costumes always had matching crowns and tiaras. That URL wasn't taken and officially became mine and I officially became *Princess* Farhana. Once my site went live, I started touring, first in the United States, then internationally. I realized that at the point I'd gotten my first reading, I'd assumed he'd meant I should change my legal name as opposed to my stage name!

Score five points for Jim Diehl.

** ** **

Sadly, Jim Diehl passed away in 2017. He was so gifted and very cordial. During one session, I asked him if he was born with his abilities. He answered no but said his grandmother had been psychic her whole life. Apparently, he'd been holding her hand as she passed and felt a bolt of lightning go up his arm. Boom! After that, he had The Sight.

Rest In Power.

IT'S IN THE CARDS

When I was small child, I desperately wanted to be a witch, a fortuneteller, or both. As a kindergartener, I'd sit on my Ukrainian grandmother's lap, listening to stories she'd tell about her mother, my great Grandma Rose. Apparently, Grandma Rose read tea leaves, as did my Aunt Alice, who, even in her seventies was still described as "a wild flapper". When I was tiny, she'd come to visit. Rotund and jovial, Aunt Alice had jet black hair, a broad cushiony bosom and sparkly crystal necklaces. Other than the crimson Prohibition era Cupid's Bow lip she still painted on, her appearance bore no resemblance to the scandalous young woman in the professional photos she'd posed for in the 1920s. Clad in nothing but a sumptuously embroidered, fringed piano shawl artfully draped around her nude body, Aunt Alice looked positively bohemian, her eyes twinkling with a come-hither look under her Louise Brooks bob. As a young woman she had that exotic *gitana* look, but as far as I knew, she *played* cards but didn't read them. Since Grandma Rose passed away several years before I was born, I never had a chance to learn how to read tea leaves from either of them.

By the age of thirteen, I was so obsessed with Tarot cards, I vowed to get some and learn how to interpret them. The only problem was nobody I knew had any firsthand experience at all-whether interpreting the cards or even from getting a reading. I'd been introduced to Tarot through h the carnival that came through the small town I lived in; there were always fortunetelling tents on the midway. Out front, hand painted banners framed by globe lights featured images of playing cards and a crude caricature of the psychic on duty, usually Romani gypsy or a wizard in a robe and a turban.

On trips to New York City to get school clothes at Best & Company, there was a storefront fortuneteller on every block. Sandwich boards set up just in front of each doorway advertised "Reunites Lovers" "God-Gifted Psychic" and "Knows All, Tells All". Neon signs blinked with glowing images of palms, eyes, stars and crescent moons surrounding the words READER AND SPIRITUAL ADVISER in fancy script. The storefront windows featured displays of large crystal balls on fancy carved wood stands, surrounded by plastic flowers in cut-glass vases and chipped statues of Roman Catholic saints and The Virgin Mary. The women, obviously Romani, stood on the sidewalk in colorful floor-length full skirts and golden hoop earrings, always with an ashy cigarillo clutched in nicotine-stained fingers. They'd call out to passersby,

"Come in honey, come in! Let me *help* you!"

My Tarot obsession knew no bounds. I did chores around the neighborhood: babysitting, mowing lawns, raking leaves, shoveling snow. Unlike the other girls in my junior high class, I didn't care that much about spending money on "cute clothes". Mine were always what would now be called vintage, bought for pennies at garage sales, so I saved up until I had enough to purchase a Tarot deck by mail order. I remember wrapping a small stack of dollar bills in a piece of white onion skin typing paper onto which I'd carefully printed my name and address. It seemed like it took ages for them to arrive. When I finally received them, I opened the box and lovingly held the cards, feeling like I was the owner of a treasure chest full of priceless jewels.

In the early 1970s, Tarot books were ridiculously hard to come by for a young teenager living in a small, mostly Catholic New England town. Undaunted, I read (and stole) books on magic from the local library, trying to find out as much as I could about this ancient divination system. Almost immediately, I started doing readings for my girlfriends. Since I didn't understand the meanings of each card, I took cues from the pictures, reciting what I thought they meant. Much to my chagrin, the derogatory nickname bestowed upon me by my classmates was "Witchiepoo", lifted from the popular *H.R. Pufnstuf* television series. Though I was an outcast at school, I didn't let that stop me from continuing my esoteric interests.

I got more books by mail order, including *Potions and Spells in Witchcraft* and Eden Gray's *Mastering The Tarot: Lessons In An Ancient Mystic Art*, through which I discovered what each card meant. I did spells and read cards avidly for years after that, until I became a young adult. My Tarot practice slowly faded into the background, replaced with the responsibilities of a grownup life: day jobs, relationships, family obligations and eventually, my wild rock'n'roll lifestyle.

After moving to Los Angeles in 1975, as a teenager, I worked as the box office girl at the famed Whisky A Go-Go, published a Xeroxed punk fanzine and started writing for the *LA Weekly* and a number of mainstream music magazines. By the 1980s, I was booking punk clubs in Hollywood. I formed an all-girl band called The Screaming Sirens; we got signed and spent the next decade recording and touring; all my witchy stuff just kinda faded into the background.

As the gloss of the music industry wore off, I missed my Tarot practice and reminded myself quite often that I needed to get back into it. I hadn't seen or handle my cherished cards for ages. I didn't make good on that promise for a few more years, but when I finally did, what happened was astonishing.

Making the firm decision to recommit to the Tarot, I rampaged through my house like a crazy person, flinging open cabinets and pawing through every box in my closet, frantically looking for any of the several decks I used to own. After a while, I realized with dismay that I no longer had *any* of them. Once again, I mail ordered a pack of cards.

Later that same day, I decided I needed to do something "responsible", so I opened a drawer to look for an insurance policy I needed to renew. Inexplicably, my very first Tarot deck was sitting beneath it! I hadn't seen those cards since the mid-1980s and with several years, and many different residences, under my belt since then, I wasn't even sure if I still owned them. To this day, I still have absolutely no explanation as to how they got there. It was an incredible moment; I felt like I'd met a long-lost old friend and got teary-eyed. The next day, the same thing happened, a different deck that I also hadn't seen for ages, appeared under a package of elastic in a box of sewing supplies…that I used on a regular basis. There was no reason for the cards to be sitting in the sewing kit, and I definitely hadn't put them there myself. This went on all week long, and by the time the cards I'd ordered arrived, I'd rediscovered six decks of my own Tarot cards, no two the same.

Obviously, I took this as a sign that I was on the right path.

BLACK DOG

Super sloppy in the back of a cab, Daniel and I were laughing, screaming, and spilling the drink I'd smuggled out of the club in my purse. The bottom halves of our faces were covered in smeared lipstick clown grins from making out wildly before, and after, we got into the taxi. We were on our way home from the notorious Club Sucker, run by famous drag queen Vaginal Crème Davis. Located in the pre-gentrified Silverlake neighborhood of Los Angeles, Sucker was packed to the rafters every Sunday. The club went from 3:00pm-9:00pm and even later if they had bands playing. The club's tagline was "Punk Rock And Show Tunes", but that was just what was advertised. It *really* should've been Day Drinking, Bathroom Bumps, Weird Hook Ups In The Alley And Cute Bartenders Who Give Away Free Drinks While Selling Drugs On The Side.

In true late Nineties fashion, Daniel and I were ridiculously messed up on a mix of ecstasy, vodka and insane amounts of cocaine, which always felt so sexy, we'd taken to calling it Love Me. After the third time the driver shot us a dirty look in the rearview mirror, we pulled it together... mainly because we didn't want to get thrown out of the cab in the shitty part of town we were in, the crime-ridden Rampart District. We rolled through the next few blocks in silence, and then the night went south.

For the past few minutes I'd noticed a large black dog bounding along the lawns of the houses we were passing. It could've been a wolf; it was bigger than a coyote but was so black, it looked like a rip in the space and time continuum. The dog had the lithe, streamlined body of a German Shepherd but much larger; the shoulders were broad, the hindquarters powerful. It paced the cab, matching the car's speed so effortlessly, it was astounding. I briefly thought of Hellhounds, the demonic black canines associated with the crossroads and The Devil himself. In legends from many cultures, seeing a Hellhound is an omen of death. I was cognizant of how ridiculously high I was, but also understood without a single doubt that the black canine was not a hallucination.

I was about to point it out to Daniel, but at that exact moment, it leaped in front of the cab so quickly, eyes flashing red in the high beams, that the driver couldn't possibly avoid it. He swerved sharply, but there was a sickening thud as the vehicle hit the dog. Whipping my head around, I saw it loping off to the side of the road before disappearing into the bushes.

"Can you pull over please?" I asked the driver, trying to stifle the hysteria in my voice.

His raised his eyes sternly into the mirror once again, flatly answering no.

"Please, can we just check to see if the dog is ok? Leave the meter on, we'll pay you!"

This time, eyes glued to the road, the driver shook his head emphatically.

"It's only an animal," he said, as though hitting a living creature was no big deal.

The second we got into Daniel's place, the tears I'd been holding in for the remainder of the ride came pouring out like a torrent of sorrow. In a trembling voice I asked him if he thought the dog was going to be ok; he pointed out that we'd both seen it running away. Still weeping, I wondered aloud if we should take another cab back up to where the accident occurred to see if the dog was injured.

Daniel held me, shushing me like a baby as I sobbed, soaking the sheets on the unmade bed. After a few minutes, he stood up wordlessly and lit a cigarette, smoking it in silence with his back to me before getting into the shower.

To call our relationship complex would be a vast understatement. It was light years beyond any "It's Complicated" situation. To begin with, I was forty-two and had been married twice. He was twenty-six and had lived with his parents before coming to America to go to art school. He was European, from Switzerland; because of our age and cultural differences, our shared frame of reference was not altogether *optimal*. But aside from that, our chemistry was so hot it was combustible, we laughed constantly. Speaking of *combustible*, the first night Daniel came to my house, as we rolled around on my living room couch, the lamp on the end table exploded. Shards of glass went everywhere, and Daniel had to leap up to extinguish the flames on the burning lampshade, finally bringing it outside to douse it with the garden hose.

We were also psychically connected. Once we had a shared dream: In my dream, I was gasping for breath, taking huge gulps of air. I woke up to the sounds of Daniel, who'd fallen asleep on the couch, wheezing in the same labored cadence. As he awoke, we both related the exact scenario, finishing each other's sentences. Another time, we were in a huge argument on the phone. After slamming down the landline receiver, I fled to my sister Eddie's house for sympathy. After a while, she suggested going to a dive bar. She decided on The White Horse Tavern, which neither of us had ever been to, purposely picking it because wasn't one of the places Daniel and I frequented. Seated at the bar a couple of Cosmopolitans in, my sister looked up from our conversation; she seemed startled.

"What the fuck is Daniel doing here?" she whispered furtively. Eyeing me suspiciously, she continued,

"Did you *tell* him we were coming here?"

I replied that didn't have a clue what she was talking about…then I looked towards the front entrance. He stood in the middle of the doorway, surveying the bar. Legs apart, hands on his hips, he looked like a cowboy reaching for his shootin' irons, about to start a gun fight.

"Let's ditch out the back door!" Eddie hissed, ducking her head and grabbing our purses.

Somehow, he didn't see us leave.

** ** **

Daniel and I met at an exquisitely trashy dive bar called The Blacklite on Valentine's Day. The attraction between us was immediate and so intense it was impossible to ignore. We probably would've thrown ourselves onto the floor and fucked right there in the middle of the bar, if it wasn't for the fact that I was completely obsessed with the person who introduced us…and *he* was infatuated with Daniel.

Larry was one of my closest friends; we were soulmates; I'd actually met him at The Blacklite. We enjoyed each other's company immensely, with endless conversations that went from highly intellectual to exploding into uproarious laughter over hot gossip. Even though he was gay, we'd spend hours at parties, in clubs and at my house kissing each other like a straight couple newly in love. He was also Daniel's art school professor.

That Valentine's Day was the Gateway Drug to an unintentionally polyamorous triangulation that lasted half a decade. Speaking of *poly*, we were all enthusiastic poly-substance users at the time and that only served to fuel our three-way fire. You name it, we experienced it as well as perpetrated it: from hot sex to coldhearted lies, from tenderness and inspiration to violence and psychological torture. The boundaries were never defined...like *at all,* in any way, shape or form. They were much more fluid than our fluid sexuality and seemed to change hourly. Though we all knew *most* of what went on, each one of us was guilty of withholding information, avoiding the truth and keeping secrets. While some of this actually had good intentions, like not wanting to hurt somebody else's feelings, it also led to trust issues as well as emotional outbursts that had the intensity of a nuclear bomb. There were several quite lengthy periods of time when one of us refused to speak to the other two.

On the night of The Black Dog Incident, Larry and I had been totally incommunicado for weeks. At that point, I wasn't sure if Daniel was talking to him...but I didn't *ask,* either. The second Daniel stepped into the shower on the Black Dog night, all I wanted to do was call Larry, but I was too emotionally exhausted to explain what had gone on that night because I was coming down off everything I'd ingested. Also, I couldn't remember what, specifically, had caused the Cold War with Larry, so there was *that.*

A day or two later, Larry called to say he missed me, asking if we could get together without Daniel. Naturally, I agreed. He suggested we meet at The Blacklite seconds before nixing it. Like my sister, Larry wanted to go somewhere Daniel didn't frequent, and Daniel and I had first met at The Blacklite – for all three of us, it was Our Bar. We settled on Frank 'n' Hank, a dive rumored to have been Charles Bukowski's favorite hangout.

Decades before Rideshare apps were a thing, taxis were really expensive. They also took eons to arrive. But even though I got wasted out of my gourd on a regular basis, I absolutely refused to drive impaired. Back then, my mantra was, "If I can't afford a cab, I can't afford a DUI". Because I had obligations the next day, I drove my black 1964 Comet Caliente convertible to Frank 'n' Hank to insure I wouldn't drink or do any of the Love Me that Larry always had on hand. Anyway, Larry loved riding in that car, he swore it made him feel like a Movie Star. He said that before he knew it was mine, he'd spotted it speeding down Sunset Boulevard with the top down and a "beautiful couple" inside, the woman's long hair blowing in the wind.

"It was so glamourous, the most *Hollywood* thing I'd ever even seen!", he said, gesturing enthusiastically with the hand that held his ever-present Parliament.

"Then I realized it was you and Daniel…", he said his voice trailing off.

** ** **

A thick pall of cigarette smoke hung in the air at Frank 'n' Hank; beneath the fluorescent lights in the back, a roaring game of pool was in session. Larry walked in so tall and handsome that all the barflies turned to stare; he certainly didn't need my car to look like a Movie Star. We hugged for a long time before sitting down. As usual, our conversation covered so many interesting topics that the hours flew by. The clock behind the bar struck midnight and regretfully, like a rock'n'roll strumpet version of Cinderella, I told him I had to get home.

As we walked to the car, I gave Larry the lowdown on the Black Dog incident in great detail. Turning the key in the ignition, the Comet's V8 engine roared to life. Since it was past midnight on a weeknight and Western Avenue was deserted, I peeled out of the parking spot, gunning down the street as I finished telling Larry the story. Less than a minute or two after I was done, once again, the night went south.

In a flash, a massive, pitch black wolf-like dog charged into the street from right to left, a few feet ahead of the car. I slammed my foot on the brake so quick and hard, the tires squealed like a girl in a horror movie. As I lost control of the two thousand pounds of Detroit steel I was driving, the Comet fishtailed wildly before stopping on a slant in the middle of the pavement, between the lanes.

In shock and hyperventilating, with both my hands still clutching the wheel, I finally realized that hadn't hit the dog. Through the windshield, I saw it streaking down the sidewalk on the driver's side of the car about half a block ahead of where we'd stopped. I glanced at Larry and his face was pallid, as though all the blood had drained out of it. After a few seconds, he gently recommended that I pull the car over. As soon as I did, I started bawling.

"How is it *possible*?" I whimpered, snot bubbling from both nostrils.

"How can that happen…*why* did it happen?"

Larry chain smoked with a blank, faraway look as though he was still trying to comprehend the events of the past fifteen minutes. Not that there was *any* sense to be made of what had just happened. We sat for a few minutes before I finally wiped my eyes, blew my nose and started the engine. Larry's apartment was close; a straight shot down Western, and block south of Wilshire, at the corner of Eighth and Gramercy.

Still shaky with adrenalin and the psychotic synchronicity that had just occurred, I drove with extreme caution, like a granny. The light was red at Wilshire; I carefully slowed to a full stop. A colossal fuel truck approached the intersection from the west, barreling down the empty street at an alarming rate. Without slowing down, it blew the red, hanging a left onto Western. The wheels screeched as the truck got so close to my car, I thought we were going to die. At that instant, a hub cap flew off one of the tremendous tires, rocketing far up into the air before swooping downwards like a gargantuan high-speed steel frisbee. Instinctually, Larry and I ducked seconds before it smashed into the left front end of The Comet.

I was out of my body, my breathing quick and shallow; my ears roaring. Both Wilshire and Western were deserted as we sat through the light changing from green to red and back again. After what seemed like an awfully long time, Larry got out to look at the front end. It appeared the only damage was a deep dent in the radiator grill where the hubcap impacted. In a soothing voice, like a hypnotist, Larry cajoled me to drive, reminding me that his house was just around the corner. Still feeling like I was floating above what was happening in *real life,* I drove the short distance in a daze.

In slow motion, I turned on Eighth Street, parking at the corner of Gramercy. Asking if I wanted to come in, I nodded dumbly as Larry got out of the car, pushing the door closed; because of its weight, he accidentally slammed it so hard that the entire vehicle shook. Still in a trance-like state, I swung my legs out, stood up shakily and closed my driver's side door softly. The second the door hinge clicked into place, the streetlight directly behind the Comet blew out with a loud, high-pitched sizzle as shards of glass rained down onto the sidewalk. *Not this, not my EPK ...please not right now!* I was so beyond traumatized at that point that I was afraid I was going to put out the power on the entire block.

I stood by the side of the car, wailing,

"Why does this stuff always happen to me?"

Larry was already sitting on the steps in the middle of grand main entrance to his building, chain smoking and waiting for me to join him. The curvilinear Art Deco apartment house had been built to resemble an ocean liner, but in the state I was in, it looked as flimsy and unrealistic as a quickly constructed set in a classic Hollywood musical. Everything seemed fake: the cars parked on the street, the dew on the lawn by the sidewalk, the mist that was forming around the blown-out streetlight. I felt like I'd entered an alternate reality, and in a way, I suppose I had. I took two steps towards Larry before collapsing on the muddy, patchy grass, sank to my knees and once again, wept hysterically. After some time, I caught my breath, smearing eyeliner all over my face as wiped my tears away. Then I half-crawled, half-stumbled up the stairs to where Larry was sitting. Wordlessly, he handed me one of his Parliaments, lighting it. Putting his arm around me, he stroked my hair the way a mother would comfort a small child after a nightmare. We sat in silence for a very long time, until the predawn light turned pale lavender.

HAPPY NEW YEAR FROM BEYOND

During the days in 1999 leading up to The New Millennium, like many people, I began reflecting on life. I thought back on the historical events I'd witnessed, the personal goals I'd achieved and everything I still wanted to accomplish, plus all the people I loved, both living and dead. What really seemed to really dominate my thoughts were the many significant relationships I had with family, friends and paramours. I was blessed with so much nurture and support. I thought of the many special people who were there for me no matter what; the ones who shared their lives with me, gave me unconditional affection and influenced my creative and artistic endeavors. One of these individuals was my close friend and belly dance mentor, the late Zein Abdul Al Malik.

Zein was a dancer of prodigious talent. Well over six feet tall and lanky, he had piercing green eyes and performed draped in billowing genie pants and luxurious folkloric garb, wrapped in antique Assuit, a traditional Egyptian mesh fabric with small strips of silver hammered into it to form designs. Zein looked imposing and exotic, like a hot genie straight out of a bottle; he was pure magic when he danced, balancing a huge brass tray laden with a full North African tea set and burning candles upon his regal head.

His career began in the San Francisco Bay Area in the mid Seventies, dancing with one of the mothers of contemporary belly dance, Jamilla Salimpour. He went on to live in Morocco and Saudi Arabia, where he resided in one of the royal palaces, thanks to his

Saudi prince lover. Zein lived and breathed Oriental Dance, performing, teaching and doing research.

After we met in 1990, he took me under his wing, *me, a beginning baby belly dancer with barely any skills*, but somehow, he saw my potential and encouraged me. Zein would have me over to his apartment, a wonderful, mysterious enclave of antique furniture inlaid with mother of pearl, luxurious plants and relics from the Middle East.

He'd make fresh mint tea in a silver Moroccan teapot, and we'd spend hours together while he showed me steps and technique, discussed belly dance traditions, and watched vintage clips he'd taped from the television in Saudi Arabia, featuring films from the 1940s and 1950s Egyptian Golden Age Of Cinema, starring famous dancers like Naima Akef, Samia Gamal and Tahiyya Carioca.

Zein also helped me select costumes, heartily encouraged my dancing, and got me my very first dance job at Hollywood's Moun Of Tunis Restaurant, where he worked. I wound up being the House Dancer there for thirty years, exactly half my lifetime.

Appropriate music for Middle Eastern dance was hard to find in America in the '90s, so Zein made me many Arabic mix tapes, which were like gold to me. Remember, there was no such thing as CDs, let alone digital downloads, back then. The cassettes he made were marvelous, featuring everything from classic live Om Kalthoum performances to the latest in Egyptian pop and Algerian *Rai* music. Every cassette Zein made also had a special cover that he thoughtfully put together by hand. Some featured Middle Eastern clipart, while others had photocopies of vintage Turkish cigarette boxes or photos of famous 1970s belly dancers like Nagwa Fouad and Soheir Zaki.

Tragically, Zein died five years after I met him. By that time, we were super close friends and gigging together regularly. I was *devastated.* I remember speaking, or rather blubbering through a speech, at his memorial, my face wet with flowing tears, but don't recall a thing I said.

I thought of him often, daily, hourly, so many things reminded me of him. At gigs whenever I felt pre-show jitters, I'd think of the way he'd calm my nerves through his twisted humor right before we both went on. Wrapped in a turban and wearing a brocade *galibiya*, shimmying to warm up, with an ever-present Marlboro in his mouth, Zein would sense my anxiety, catch my eye, make an exaggerated coquettish gesture then and whisper in a feminine falsetto,

"How's my hair?"

Somehow, our private joke never got old, always making me laugh hysterically. Whenever he did that, I had a great show, entering the stage with a huge grin on my face. Even though Zein's been departed for decades, I *always* think of him just before I go on.

On New Year's Eve 1999, at five minutes of midnight, I was at a belly dance gig, in the dressing room, wearing a brand new costume I'd made, *my first costume for the New Millennium.*

The dancer I was working with asked what music I was planning to perform to for my first dance set of the new century.

"I don't know!" I sighed, wildly pawing through my CD binder, "I'm so *sick* of all my music!"

My gig bag was full of the usual belly dance accouterments: stray finger cymbals, perfume, hair accessories, dirty ballet slippers, mis-matched sequin armbands, loose aspirin tablets, safety pins.

Suddenly, something fell into my hands, a small plastic case. Though my suitcase was always chaotic, there was a method to my madness, and it was always re-packed before every show. The little plastic box was decidedly an unfamiliar object that I didn't remember adding. Recognizing what it was in the dim dressing room lighting by the feel of it alone, I wondered how it got there.

"Hey, no way, there's a *cassette* in my dance bag!" I cried, kind of amazed.

"You still use *cassettes*?" the other dancer asked incredulously.

"Well, no, not for years", I answered, dumbfounded,

"I have no idea what it's doing in here!"

"Maybe we can dance to it," she said, "What is it?"

I glanced at the clock-it was now exactly one minute before midnight.

Thinking we'd better figure our music out immediately, I flipped the mystery cassette case over in my hands. The cover featured a black and white drawing of a 1920s flapper lounging in a champagne glass.

In hand-lettered Art Deco font, it read:

"HAPPY NEW YEAR!

LOVE, ZEIN"

As the clock struck twelve and the new century began, I got chills.

RENDEZVOUS IN CAIRO

The kid was all arms and legs, with curly jet-black hair and teeth that were so gleaming white, they looked like a set of expensive veneers from a Beverly Hills cosmetic dentist. Oblivious to his teenage good looks, it was obvious he'd reach Heartbreaker Status within the next two years. Though I noticed his appearance, it wasn't what initially attracted me to him. I picked him out of the crowd of the hundreds of people who surrounded him because he seemed comfortable, almost familiar, and very approachable. More importantly, he exuded an air of innocence, good intentions and trustworthiness that made him stand out from everyone else. Without even thinking about it, I knew he was the right person for the little favor I needed.

I'd arrived in Cairo barely five hours ago and was in The Manic Phase Of Jetlag. Since sleeping was fucking impossible, the only sane thing to do was go out exploring. Walking for even a few minutes down the bustling streets of Cairo is always interesting. You never know what you'll see: it's pure sensory overload, almost like an acid trip, but real life. The moment the *muezzins* call the prayers from Cairo's hundreds of mosques, every animal in the entire city joins in for a sonic symphony. Camels bellow, donkeys and horses bray, dogs howl, sheep and goats baaa and bleat. Simultaneously, cabbies pullover in unison like a choreographed Busby Berkeley number in an old Hollywood musical. The drivers jump from their cars, rolling out rugs or placing pieces of cardboard on the street to bow down and pray. At night, thousands stroll the famous Qasr El Nil bridge watching the billowing sails of the elegant *felucca* boats float by, or the motor-powered Party Boats lit up like carnival rides, blasting Arabic pop and techno at deafening decibels, zigzagging from shore to shore. There are often chickens pecking around inside the elevators... or at the main post office. The streets are insane: Egyptians never pay attention to little formalities like traffic signals or One Way signs. Crossing the street is akin to putting your life on the line: if you make a mad dash and actually get to the other side, crowds of pedestrians applaud heartily.

As a professional belly dancer, I'd been going to Egypt regularly since the early 1990s, but this trip was a surprise; I hadn't expected to visit twice in 2009. It came about whirlwind style, a week before I departed. My friend Jim, an up-and-coming American male belly dancer was originally supposed to go to Egypt as part of a tour group. When it got cancelled, his plans were scotched at the last minute. Nervous about going on his own for the first time, he told me had air miles and asked if I'd accompany him in exchange for picking up my ticket. For once, my schedule was clear, so I answered by hollering *aiwa*, Arabic for "yes", so loudly he dropped his phone.

The flight from LAX to Cairo is sixteen to twenty-two hours long depending on the city you transfer through and the layover length, so arriving in Egypt absolutely trashed at 3:00am was always a foregone conclusion. By the time Jim and I checked into the Cairo Sheridan, it was almost 5:00am. Tossing and turning in my bed, I tried not to disturb him as the sunlight peeked in through the blackout shade. He asked in a whisper if I was still awake. By the time our conversation turned to disco producer Giorgio Moroder's virtuosity on the extended 12" single of Donna Summer's "I Feel Love", I knew there was no way in hell we were going to get any sleep. At the hotel's sumptuous breakfast buffet, Jim chattered excitedly about all the tourist attractions we'd see. In those days, none of the antiquities or museums were open on Friday, which is the Muslim Sabbath. He looked utterly crestfallen at the news, but I came up with a fabulous backup plan in seconds.

"We can go to *Khan Al Khalili*! It's the best *souk* ever!"

Though he knew several Arabic dance terms, Jim had no idea what *souk* meant. I explained it was Arabic for "market" and he immediately embraced The Crabby Sleep Deprived Phase Of Jetlag, his face wrinkling into an expression of distaste.

"You don't understand," I said sincerely,

"Wait'll we get there, you'll see!"

Khan El Khalili is perhaps the most famous *bazaar* in all of North Africa and the Middle East. Located in the center of Islamic Cairo, it is adjacent to the intricate minarets of the nearby Al Hussain Mosque. The covered marketplace was built in 1174, becoming a booming international trade center during the Mamluk Sultanate. Camel caravans on the Spice Route always stopped there, and the name Khan Al Khalili was appropriated from a nearby *caravanserai* or inn, where merchants and their pack animals could rest for the night.

A magical vortex melding the Middle Ages with the Twenty First Century, the juxtaposition of old and new is staggering. Soaring limestone archways provide the entrance to a twisted warren of tiny lanes crammed with oriental rugs, stained glass lanterns, camel saddles and carved wooden boxes inlaid with nacre. Tremendous burlap sacks full of cumin, aniseed and coriander sit in front of the shops, their fragrances mingling with the scents of neroli, jasmine and myrrh emanating from delicate blown glass perfume bottles.

Little boys carrying metal trays of mint tea and Coca-Cola scurry around delivering refreshments to the merchants and their customers, each side bargaining furiously at the top of their lungs. In the jewelry s*ouk,* 22 Karat cartouches customized with tourists' names share cases with Edwardian era serpent rings, their scales made of black diamonds with emeralds for eyes. Traditionally made Papyrus scrolls painted with hieroglyphics and images of Bastet or the goddess Isis were stacked in neat piles. Trashed speakers blasted *shaabi* (the urban Egyptian equivalent of hip hop) from stalls selling everything from surprisingly slutty lingerie and plastic children's toys to electronics, Chinese designer knockoffs and glittering handmade belly dance costumes. At the famous Fishawy's Café, elderly bearded men wearing turbans play backgammon for hours at outdoor tables, trying to ignore the nubile Eastern European girls in scanty halter tops having their first taste of Arabic coffee.

Jim and I exit our cab, immediately sucked into the congested madness Of *Sharia Al Muski* aka Market Street. Colorful hand-sewn canopies, blinking lights and clotheslines heavy with laundry are strung from building to building over cobblestone streets jammed with taxis, tour buses and donkey carts laden with vegetables. Families of four crammed onto a moped cut through lanes at warp speed; a woman swathed in black veils sways down the street carrying a baby on one hip, with a huge faux Gucci tote atop her head. Mini vans empty out like clown cars while Cairo City Buses barely stop, the passengers leaping off them like stage divers at a punk show. Delivery men balancing gigantic trays stacked with loaves of bread on their heads whiz by on bicycles as pedestrians jump out of the way. A tour group takes photos of a man in a *Saidi* headwrap and traditional *galabeya* riding by on a gigantic camel...while loudly conversing on his mobile phone.

Taking it all in, Jim is stupefied, standing perfectly still. He's just entered The Culture Shock Phase Of Jetlag. Suddenly, he snaps out of it, furiously rifling through his wallet, pulling out a card.

"Hey, I think Ahmed has a shop here!" he yells jubilantly,

"He always says to look him up if we're in Cairo... let's find it!"

We know Ahmed from the belly dance workshop circuit in the States; he's a popular vendor at dance festivals. An Egyptian raised in the UK, Ahmed speaks at least three languages, chain smokes like a motherfucker, has a sardonic sense of humor and always gives us discounts. It would be great to see him.

Jim squints at the card, cocking his head with a perturbed look on his face.

"Hmmm...all it says is 'New Khan Al Khalili Bazaar'-there's no address on here, what the fuck?"

I assure him that there are no addresses anywhere in the *souk*; they're not needed. The buildings are so old they don't even have numbers posted, and anyway, all you have to do is ask someone.

"Just *ask* someone?" Jim challenges,

"How are you going to find someone who speaks English? What are you going to do, go from person to person for hours until you find someone who knows him? Are you kidding me?"

It was abundantly clear that that Jim had gone directly from The Culture Shock Phase Of Jetlag right into The Entitled American Phase Of Jetlag, skipping a few phases entirely. His eyes darted around wildly, surveying the roiling masses of humanity surrounding us.

"Yeah, I'll just find someone who speaks English and knows Ahmed," I shrugged. I knew I could do it.

While Jim wrung his hands like Margaret Dumont playing an aging High Society Dowager in a Marx Brothers film, I took a quick scan of the crowd. A watermelon pink t-shirt caught my attention from about fifty feet away, and I said triumphantly,

"*That* person speaks English, I'm sure of it!"

Jim clutched my hand tightly as I dragged him through the teaming crowd. He kept repeating like a mantra: *What are we doing?*

What makes you think this random person speaks English?

This is insane...YOU are insane!

I stopped about four feet away from the kid in the pink t-shirt, who was talking to a friend. I stared until he felt it, and he looked at me quizzically, his body language asking *What do you want?*

In my toddler-level Arabic, I asked,

"Min fadlak, kalam angalizi?" (translation: Please, talk English?)

"Yes, I speak English."

I handed him the card; he glanced at it. Then, with what could only be described as a slapstick double take, he stared sat it again, as though he was reading something he couldn't understand...and maybe he really couldn't. It is entirely possible that a person who spoke fluently in either language couldn't read the second language because both alphabets are completely different...and Ahmed's card was printed in English.

The kid took a step towards me, his big brown Bambi eyes growing huge for a second before he tilted his head, narrowing his eyes asking almost suspiciously,

"Why you give me this?"

"Because I want to go there," I said slowly and deliberately, thinking maybe his English was on the same level as my Arabic, continuing,

"Ahmed is my friend."

"But *why*?" the kid asked again, taking another step closer,

"Why you give *me* this?"

Before I could answer, he blurted out,

"This my shop!"

"Oh come *on*," I said.

It crossed my mind he might've been one of the older delivery boys and was trying to scam me. He'd probably take me to…like…his fat old uncle's stall and try to get me "a deal" on a shitty soapstone King Tut statuette.

"Lady!" the kid cried, snapping me out of it, "This my shop! *This Mister Ahmed's shop… I take you now*!

With that, he grabbed my hand and started pulling me along, walking quickly and then almost sprinting. We wended our way through the maze-like configuration of skinny alleys as Jim tried to keep up with our pace. We passed by souvenir statues of various Egyptian gods before getting into a less touristy area loaded with shiny, hammered copper pots and pans before taking a detour into several stalls loaded with brightly embroidered Bedouin robes…then bridal shops displaying bolts of bejeweled lace and sparkly fabric. At this point, Jim was almost in a fugue state, huffing and puffing.

"This is getting dangerous!" he cried, entering The Deliriously Sleepy Tourist Stage Of Jetlag.

"We should go back!" he said anxiously, "I *really* don't like this!"

I yelled back that the worst thing that could possibly happen is that we'd get stuck for twenty minutes or so, haggling over pyramid shaped souvenir key chains.

The kid took a quick turn, and surprisingly, we were in a contemporary air-conditioned building. Every stall featured glass cases piled high with sterling silver jewelry. Releasing my hand, the kid bolted into one of the shops, shouting at the top of his lungs in rapid fire staccato, gesticulating wildly. Due to my limited Arabic, I could only make out the phrase he repeated over and over: *Mish mumkin,* which means, "It is not possible".

Through a window hung with a curtain of silver pendants and chains, I saw Ahmed rise from a chair behind the counter. I could barely believe my eyes. Seconds later, Ahmed noticed Jim and me, his eyes growing wide with shock, just as the kid's had a few minutes ago. Ahmed motioned us to come in, simultaneously snapping his fingers, flagging down a delivery boy to get us mint tea and cake.

"*Marhaba* Princess Farhana and Jim," he said, using my stage name. The moment the kid heard my name, he shot me a quick glance, shaking his head almost imperceptibly.

Pulling out chairs, Ahmed lit a cigarette, motioning us to sit down before fixing his gaze on me.

"So…you just walk up to 'Slam in the middle of a street full of people, show him my card and ask him to take you to my shop?"

"Yes, I replied.

Exhaling a long stream of smoke, Ahmed nodded slowly, considering my answer carefully, as though he was making a judgment.

Still staring at me, he raised an eyebrow, enquiring,

"You are *Pisces*?"

Surprised he guessed my sign, I nodded affirmatively as a knowing, Mona Lisa smile crossed Ahmed's face.

"I am also Pisces", he said, as Jim and 'Slam stared in mute amazement. Ahmed continued,

"All Pisces, we are *psychic*!", he declared, pronouncing it sick-ick.

Everyone was silent for a few seconds, and then I noticed an orange tabby cat lying in the glass case on top of a mound of silver jewelry, suckling four tiny kittens.

"Wow," I said absolutely charmed, "Your cat and her babies look so comfortable, and she's so beautiful. What's her name?"

Ahmed started laughing, shaking his head.

'Slam, short for Islam, let out a giggle before saying,

"If you come in here like...like...*normal* person, you would not believe! But now I think you see it is very, very *mumkin*! Aiwa, like you, the cat, she is beautiful... and her name is also Princess".

GET YOUR KICKS ON ROUTE 666

My sister, my daughter…my daughter, my sister…

She's my sister-and my daughter!

I was standing on my kitchen steps in a t-shirt and panties at 6:00am, punctuating my hysterics by slapping myself across the face and I had absolutely *no idea* why I felt the need to be play-acting the most infamous scene from Roman Polanski's 1974 neo-noir hit "Chinatown". For some unknown reason, I'd woken up with this frenzy, in minute detail, running through my head. It was almost as though I was being manipulated by some unseen force.

My new boyfriend Pa regarded me affectionately, and a little curiously, as he handed me a cup of coffee.

"What are you doing?" he asked affably, as though this wasn't such unusual display at the crack of dawn.

I explained that I was acting out both the Faye Dunaway and Jack Nicholson parts from the scene where Evelyn Mulray, under duress from sadistic private dick Jake Gittes, breaks down and admits to the incest in her family.

"Oh," he said, nodding as though this was a perfectly logical answer,

"I never saw *Chinatown,* but I heard it was good!"

There was a reason Pa wasn't fazed by my behavior. Even though we were in the throes of new love, we'd actually known each other for ages and had a lot of history together. We'd met in the 1990s at the now-legendary Clown Party, an epic private even held at the Phoenix Iron Works warehouse in Oakland, California. Hundreds of people from every facet of the Bay Area's alternative scene attended: punks, visual and performance artists, skateboarders, college students and mad scientists from Survival Research Labs, all dressed like clowns. Pretty much the whole party was tripping their brains out on massive amounts of the freshly picked psilocybin mushrooms that the host had thoughtfully left out as party favors. Like any rational, well-adjusted person, I *detested* clowns. But one glance at Pa, handsome in his crisp painstakingly applied whiteface and a professional-looking red nose changed that. He was the sexiest clown I had ever seen. The following day, sans make up, he was even sexier. He had a dangerous, brooding Bad Boy appeal and a beautiful smile. I was beyond smitten...also, I had a *husband*.

Pa's real name was James. "Pa" was an old Army moniker, an abbreviation that had come from the first two letters of his last name. He'd been stationed in various Asian jungles for two years, and after being discharged he'd come to San Francisco to attend art school. It was a hot combination, he was a robust, ripped alpha male who could carry on conversations about classical literature and art theory. Though he'd grown his crewcut out into a long, braided rat-tail that fell to his hips, some of his Army habits died hard; he was never without combat boots and still wore a bandanna tied around his head pirate-style, something he'd picked up Thailand to prevent leaches from crawling into his ears while he slept on the ground. He'd tell insane stories about getting fully suited up in HAZMAT suits and gas masks during all-night chemical drills and taking LSD to stay awake.

Whenever I'd come up to the Bay Area, he'd make special trips from his little ranch in Sonoma to see me, but nothing ever happened, so I couldn't tell if he felt the same about me. We'd get shit-faced at Oakland dive bars like Esther's Orbit Room, but all we ever did was hold hands. Besides, both of us had always been with other people. When he married suddenly and disappeared, I was heartbroken. More than decade later I still thought of him constantly, so I worked my romantic demons out by writing a story about him called "Coco The Zombie Clown From Heaven", which was published in my memoir collection, *Escape From Houdini Mountain.*

In early 2002, years after his wife died and long after he'd broken up with the girlfriend who followed her, Pa was living in New Mexico. Someone had given him my book as a gift, asking if the story was about him. He read it and found me immediately, less than four months before the "Chinatown" moment unfolded.

For once, our timing was perfect, he was single, and I was just beginning to get over a cougar-iffic love affair with a Euro-trash artist fifteen years my junior. I was excited, but also extremely gun-shy. James had meant so much to me for so long, that the first time he came out to visit me, I decided I wasn't going to sleep with him. No matter what happened, it would undoubtedly end badly, if it was awful, it would ruin our friendship; if it was great, I would be more in love than I already was. Because he lived in a different state, that would suck.

I held out for exactly seventeen hours.

Naturally, we slept together and of course it was amazing. The next morning, I was appearing as the principle dancer in a video for a hip-hop artist called Truth Hurts. Her song "Addictive" had Arabic and Indian samples in it, and I'd been hired to belly dance in the club scene. Because it was my birthday, I made the executive decision to bring Pa to the set with me; something I'd never done before. When we arrived at the location, we were surprised to see stars like Snoop Dog, Dr. Dre, Eric B and Rakim, all of whom were making cameo appearances. The set was so thick with reefer smoke it was like a 'hood version of a Cheech And Chong movie, only it was real. The makeup artist had to come around every five minutes to drop Visine into the bloodshot eyes of the guest stars... it was *that* bad. After the shoot, we were as inseparable as was humanly possible, given our long-distance romance. The reason Pa and I were awake so early that "Chinatown" morning was because we were about to embark on a road trip back to his place in Santa Fe.

Pa loaded up his new ride, a dilapidated 1970s pick-up truck, riddled with rust, its hideous yellow ochre paint sun-bleached and dotted with liberal amounts of Bondo and primer. The truck's deck had a makeshift bed, a rotten piece of foam covered by old moving blankets, and was crowned with an ugly, decomposing brick-red camper shell, awash with Fiberglass splinters. People were always giving Pa vehicles that were destined for the junkyard, and he'd drive them into the ground with screw drivers stuck into the ignition, their engines literally held together with plastic zip-ties from garbage bags. After making a picnic of sandwiches and snacks, I threw my computer and a baby blue duffle bag full of cosmetics, high heels and slutty undies into the backseat, and we took off heading east on Interstate 10.

The truck hiccupped and creaked along as we laughed constantly, discussing everything from our childhoods to what had happened to mutual friends from Phoenix Iron Works. With a dog-eared map spread on my lap, I recited the odd names of the tiny desert towns we'd pass through. In no hurry at all, we planned to drive 'til we couldn't anymore and stay overnight at some shitty motel, it didn't matter where, we'd just carry on with the 1,366-mile journey at our own pace. We stopped a couple of times for Slurpees and ice cream, browsing leisurely for souvenirs at truck stops, and wandering around rest areas in the arid air, inspecting the vintage adobe Visitor Centers, marveling at massive cacti and eavesdropping on the other motorists gathered around the wind-worn picnic tables.

The periwinkle desert twilight had long turned to cool darkness by the time we pulled into Kingman, Arizona, 318 miles east of Hollywood. As Pa fueled up the truck, I admired the Atomic Age motel next to the service station, before noticing that the total of the gas purchased was $9.11. Though usually pragmatic, I've always been superstitious, and with the September 11th tragedy in the very near past, I took this number as a bad omen. It crossed my mind that it might be a prudent idea to spend the night at the motel…but dismissed the notion without mentioning it to Pa, in case he'd think I was being neurotic.

We drove off into the night, and by the time we were traveling down Highway 40, on the remnants of what used to be Route 66, we were both in hysterics regaling each other with crazy teenage stories about getting wasted on Quaaludes and Boone's Farm at house parties with absent parents, making out for hours at accompanied by Led Zeppelin's "Stairway To Heaven". The highway was utterly deserted, we were the only vehicle on the road. It was also unlit and in the pitch dark, the sky was full of stars so bright you could see them clearly through the cracked, bug-splattered windshield.

Presently, down the road in front of us, we saw a dim radiant glow. This led to a conversation about UFOs sightings. As we drew closer to the light, we realized it was coming from a gigantic truck that was spraying insecticide into the scrubby trees on the side of the road. The spewing poisonous mist formed a large cloud, illuminated by the truck's headlights as we drove past. I told Pa about Jayne Mansfield's grisly and untimely death in Mississippi on Highway 90, when a tractor trailer swerved to avoid a mosquito spraying truck, when suddenly, we heard sirens.

I'd actually noticed the parked cop car on the side of the road earlier, and assumed it had been accompanying the spraying truck, but the moment the red and blue lights began flashing, we realized we were getting pulled over. Since we weren't speeding, both of us unsure what this was about. Pa stopped the truck up on the shoulder and pulled out his license, instructing me to grab the registration from the glove box.

The cop took his time ambling up to our vehicle. The moment he shined his flashlight into the cab, he saw my nurse's hat fall out of the glove compartment.

"Ma'am" he said, "Are you a nurse?"

Staring at the cap on the floor mat with the crooked, lipstick red vinyl cross sloppily glue-gunned to it, I mumbled in real embarrassment,

"Um…no sir… I'm not a nurse."

The hat, of course, went with my bag full of slutty undies.

Shit! I thought, why *did I ignore that 911-gas pump… we should've stayed in Kingman!*

The cop directed his gaze at Pa.

"You know your license plate light is out?" he asked, as though it was a major felony.

He made both of us hand over our identification and took his sweet time calling it in. I watched the minutes ticking by on the dash clock, which miraculously, still worked, as we listened to the far-away static dispatch radio from the squad car. Finally, the officer returned, handing us both back our licenses.

He said in a monotone,

"Sir? Could you please step out of the truck?"

The moment Pa obliged, the cop swiftly bent him over the hood of the truck, clasping a set of cuffs on him with a loud clatter. I was halfway out of the truck's passenger door, already yelling, when the cop barked at me to "sit tight" and ordered me to "shut up for my own good". I watched mutely from the cab as he attached leg irons and a waist-chain that linked to Pa's handcuffs. By the time he pulled his cruiser up, throwing Pa into the back seat and slamming the door, I was out of the truck.

"What are you *doing*?" I demanded, really agitated, "What's going on?"

"I'm taking him in," the cop said, deadpan.

I was beginning to shake uncontrollably; I didn't understand what was happening, but I instinctively knew it was bad...*really bad*.

"Where are you taking him?" I shouted, starting to lose it.

"*Why* are you taking him?"

In an almost bored voice, the cop told me I really didn't need to know *why* James was getting brought in, but that they were going to the jail in Prescott, Arizona, which was about an hour away. He said I could call the jail in two hours to find out the booking status.

The cop started getting into his car, and abruptly, in spite of my emotional upset, my self-preservation instinct kicked in and my mind began to race: How *the hell could I call the jail when I didn't own a cell phone? Even if I had one, it wouldn't work out here…It would be completely impossible for me drive this jalopy for hours across the desert!*

Without even realizing what I was doing, I practically jumped onto the cop, blocking him from the driver's seat.

"You can't just *leave* me here," I wailed.

"By law, ma'am, I can" he said coldly.

"Call me a tow truck," I shrieked, "You cannot leave me in the middle of nowhere!"

"Ma'am, I don't need to do that… we are leaving-*now!*" he said adamantly.

A potent adrenalin rush engulfed me so completely that I felt like I was outside myself. Suddenly I grabbed the cop roughly by the shoulders, and in a voice I didn't even recognize as my own, got right up into his face all wild-eyed and growled,

"Give me your fucking badge number then, because when they discover me raped and murdered out here, *it's gonna be in my fucking pocket!*"

The cop stared in shock as I sprawled across the hood of the police car, gripping the open door of the drive's side, preventing him from entering, screaming over and over like a banshee,

"CALL ME A TOW TRUCK NOW!"

Realizing he couldn't go anywhere without the situation escalating even more than it already had, the cop got on the radio and called a wrecker.

When he informed me that it would take around forty-five minutes to arrive, I went ballistic again, yelling like a maniac that he had to wait for me because there was *no way I* could be left in the desert alone. My screams echoed into the empty night like a funhouse soundtrack. Rolling his eyes, the officer radioed for another cop to come and wait with me for the tow truck. The pig wouldn't let me near James, not even to speak to him. I watched him forlornly through the window in the back of the squad car. The moonlight lit up the tears welling in his eyes; as he mouthed to me, I'm *sorry*. With that, I burst into hysterical sobs.

After what seemed like ages, the other cop arrived, oddly enough, with his teenage son in tow. He stepped out of his car so both officers could have a conference. By this time, I was leaning against the back bumper of Pa's truck, tears rolling silently and steadily down my cheeks, my whole body heaving and trembling as I stared directly into the headlights of the second black and white. The lamps seemed to be dimming and getting brighter rhythmically, matching my jagged, uneven breathing. At first, I thought this was an optical illusion caused by the tears from my eyes…then the squad car's motor died.

I realized, with the deep sense of dread I always got when this sort of thing happened, that it was My Electrical Disturbance leaping into action. This might be hard for some people to comprehend, but My Electrical Disturbance, which is correctly called Electro-Psychokinesis or EPK, has plagued my entire life. I routinely freeze computers, fry cell phones, disable cameras and cash registers, go through car batteries at the rate of, like, six a year, demagnetize credit cards and can't wear a watch. It also gets very expensive…all that equipment getting ruined. My Electrical Disturbance only seems to occur when I'm extremely upset, really stressed out or very excited. When it starts happening, it used to scare me. Already stressed, I experience even *more* anxiety and want to vomit. For years I tried to keep it a secret, but it got to the point that everyone around me started noticing. Thanks to Steven King, my close friends started calling me "Carrie" and "Firestarter".

EPK is a phenomenon that hasn't been studied much, because like me, the people who are born with it usually experience it in times of extreme emotional highs or lows and generally, these actions cannot be reproduced at will, so it is impossible for researchers to collect much data on the subject.

The onset of my EPK upset me even more, but I snapped back into reality when I heard both cops arguing about the dead squad car.

"But I had it serviced this morning!" the second officer was exclaiming in frustration, "Look in the logbook! I checked *everything*!"

The tow truck, a huge red vintage flatbed, arrived. The driver jumped out, and in the midst of my breakdown, I noticed that with his shaggy hair, five o'clock shadow and hulking frame, he looked like a cross between Chuck Norris in the '70s and Sasquatch. After a pow wow with the cops, he hooked our dilapidated truck to the tow bar as the car with Pa in it took off swiftly, veering off the road and across the desert in a vortex of dust, headed for Prescott.

"Get in," the tow truck driver said to me, tilting his head towards the wrecker's cab before hollering over his shoulder to the second cop and his son,

"I'll be back for you guys in about an hour!"

As we drove in silence, I tried valiantly not to bawl out loud.

"Rough night, huh?" the driver asked in a voice that was gruff but compassionate.

I couldn't answer, so he wordlessly handed me some tissues.

Finally, we pulled into what seemed to be very small town. The driver stopped in front of squatty cement structure with a large neon sign depicting a panther: "The World Famous Black Cat Bar". Jumping out of the truck, he undid a giant padlock a in the middle of a Cyclone fence and swung open the gate to his tow yard, declaring,

"We're at the end of the line, hon!"

"Where are we?"

"Welcome to Seligman, Arizona, population 456", he said,

"There's a motel across the street, you can spend the night there. I charge $25.00 a day for vehicle storage up front...but you can just give it to me in the morning."

I decided that *now* wasn't the time tell him that I didn't have a credit card on me and was carrying only $28.00 in cash.

Grabbing my stuff from Pa's pickup, I crossed the deserted street and composing myself, checked into the Supai Motel, trying to ignore the fluorescent buzz of a burned-out light... and the suspicious look the desk clerk was giving me. I got the last room they had for $16.00 and of *course* it was Number 13. It was spartan, with indoor-outdoor carpeting, but at least it was clean.

Momentarily I thought of visiting The World Famous Black Cat Bar and getting shitfaced with my last twelve dollars. But at the rate things were going it kind of seemed like a horrible idea. Besides, I had other stuff to attend to… like using the old-school dial phone in the room to call the Prescott Jail to check on Pa's booking and getting in touch with my sister so she could wire me some money. In something akin to the early stages of schizophrenia, I became engulfed in a gigantic shame spiral. I seriously could not *believe* this chain of events was happening to me at the age of forty-three… *Wasn't this shit supposed to magically cease and desist sometime during the early twenties?*

And then there was the last task, one I really wasn't looking forward to at all; introducing myself *–for the very first time*, to Pa's mother via a frantic collect call at 1:45am. Gritting my teeth and steeling myself for the worst, I dialed her number.

Hello, is this Betty? My name is Pleasant. You don't know me, but I'm your son's girlfriend. Sorry to wake you up, but I'm stranded somewhere in the middle of Arizona, and James is in jail…

Pa had already processed through the Yavapai County Jail in Prescott, but that was the only information I could get besides the fact that they were holding him without bail and wouldn't let me speak to him. My sister wasn't home, so I left a message. The phone call with Pa's mom went, I suppose, as well as a phone call of that nature could possibly go…at least she didn't hang up on me!

By then, it was 2:30 am, too late for The Black Cat, and I sure as fuck wouldn't be able to sleep. All there was left to do was chain smoke, cry, and maybe try to numb myself by watching TV. The ancient television, with its rabbit-ear antenna, took a long time to tune in, but when the picture finally materialized showing the Channel 10 station identification logo, the announcer's deep voice boomed:

WE NOW RETURN YOU TO OUR MOVIE "CHINATOWN", STARRING JACK NICHOLSON AND FAYE DUNAWAY.

The film flickered onto to the screen at the *very* point where the "My sister.... My daughter" scene began.

All the hair on my body stood on end. I shuddered in utter disbelief, chills running up my spine. I felt like I was drowning, like my brain was being sucked slowly and loudly out of my skull. In the midst of it all, my thoughts came thick and fast.

How was this even possible…especially after the episode with My Electrical Disturbance? Why the hell hadn't I paid attention to that damn gas pump? More importantly, how come my clairvoyance had shown me "Chinatown", and not the part about the police pulling us over? What the actual fuck?

I started crying hysterically again, and at some point, still in my clothing, fell into a deep, fitful sleep. I awoke suddenly to blinding desert sunlight and the tinny sounds of ranchera music on a cheap radio, floating above the roar of the maid's vacuum cleaner in the room next door. I took a shower and tried to apply make-up over my tear-swollen eyes. I was gonna need every bit of what was left of my feminine wiles to figure out storing the truck, not to mention getting out of Seligman, considering the fact that I was twelve bucks away from being flat broke.

Grabbing a paper cup full of the brown crayon water that was masquerading as coffee in the lobby, I began trying think coherently about negotiating vehicle storage at the tow yard, not to mention financing my trip back home.

The Chuck Norris guy greeted me brusquely with a grunt as I entered his garage. He rolled out from beneath the chassis, dressed in worn, grease-stained coveralls. Lighting a Marlboro, he repeated his terms, and then asked if my boyfriend had gotten out of jail. I started weeping again, snot dribbling out of my nostrils as I recounted the previous night's events...leaving out the crazy paranormal shit so I wouldn't sound completely insane.

"Oh, man...*please* don't cry!" he begged, his demeanor changing unexpectedly,

"I just cannot *handle* seeing a woman crying!"

He pulled out a plastic orange crate, gesturing for me to sit down as he handed me a clean red chamois cloth to wipe my eyes with and a glass of water.

"You seem like a nice person", he said earnestly,

"I know you're really upset...and I'm not sure why your boyfriend is in jail..."

"I'm not either!" I wailed, lips quivering, snot bubbling out of my nostrils like a child, "They wouldn't *tell* me!"

He looked me straight in the eyes and told me he would store the truck until James got out of jail, and only charge me five bucks a day instead twenty-five, but that I had to *promise* to mail him the cash as soon as I got home. Gratefully agreeing to his terms, I offered to leave my license as collateral, but waved his hand in dismissal. Writing me up a receipt, he said a Greyhound bus came through the town, and let me use the shop phone to make a reservation. The automated voice stated that the bus only came through Seligman every three days; apparently, I'd just missed one. Seligman, known as The Birthplace Of Route 66, is located in Northern Arizona's Upland Mountains, "conveniently located" exactly 180 miles away from both Phoenix and The Grand Canyon...which was a euphemism for In The Middle Of Nowhere.

As I hung up in despair, the tow driver told me I could get a flight from Flagstaff to Phoenix, so I could then fly to LA. I reached my sister, told her the predicament, and she called back after she'd booked the flights for me. Wolfing down the Snickers bar the guy offered me after he called the taxi service, I thanked him gratefully and profusely for his kindness. Things were actually starting to look up!

The "cab" turned out to be a black 1980s Cadillac Seville with a burgundy velvet interior, arrived an hour and change later. The sunburned driver was portly in a plaid shirt, Polyester pants and a shocking white comb-over. Holding the door open for me, he told me that the journey to Flagstaff would take roughly two hours. Shaking Chuck Norris' hand, I slid into the car's front seat, and we took off.

Neil Diamond was playing softly on the radio as we drove through the barren desert. Thinking of Pa in jail, I felt tears welling up again. Staring out the window at the scrubby landscape, I tried to be as silent as possible, just for the sake of being polite.

An hour or so went by before the driver, in a timid voice, ventured,

"Miss? I know this isn't any of my business, and I don't know what happened to you, but I hope you'll be all right. I don't want to pry... but..."

Taking a measured breath, he continued,

"I wanted to let you know that... you're... the most beautiful woman I've ever had in my cab. I'm a married man, so I don't *mean anything* by this...but, uh, I want to help, so this ride is on me".

I looked over at his sincere face and burst into tears again loudly.

"Thank you so much!" I sobbed.

We drove the rest of the way in silence. When he let me out at the Flagstaff Airport he wouldn't take a tip, just patted me on the arm in a fatherly way and wished me luck. Even though the airport was the size of a postage stamp with only one runway, because the September 11 tragedy was still an open wound, the security line was a bitch.

As it happened, I had a Starred Ticket, which I soon found out meant I was singled out for "secondary search". The extremely thorough agents succeeded in knocking six keys off my brand-new laptop. Then they confiscated all the vintage diaper pins inside my bag. *Like, sure, I was totally planning to hijack the plane by brandishing a diaper pin decorated with a yellow plastic ducky!* As they did this, a woman breezed through the line wearing one of those giant American Flag pins made of beads...and twenty or thirty safety pins.

"What about *her*? "I asked indignantly. "She's got tons of safety pins on!"

"Oh, "the security agent said, "That's just *jewelry*!"

With all the security procedures, I barely made my plane, which turned out to be a single engine eight-seater. Five passengers were men, ranging from executives to desert rats, and there was a pair of newlyweds who'd obviously been honeymooning at the Grand Canyon. Their affection made me lonely for Pa and their clean-cut appearance made me envious. It was abundantly clear that neither of them had never jumped on the hood of a police car like a lunatic, experienced psychic issues involving popular films, or gotten stranded in a surreal one-horse town with no money. I felt immensely sorry for myself and during the bumpy take off, and the crying kicked in again.

I didn't even notice the incredible turbulence until the flight attendant started doling out barf bags to everyone, handing me my bag along with small package of Kleenex. As we flew directly into a vicious thunderstorm, the plane hurdled up and shot down hundreds of feet like a thrill ride. Shell shocked, I watched with a detached fascination as huge, fake-looking white bolts of lightning practically bounced off the wings. Passengers were heaving and retching loudly, and the entire cabin reeked of vomit. The new bride clutched her husband's hand, praying out loud as the pilot yelled frantically into his headset and the flight attendant white-knuckled the arm rests on her seat.

After what seemed like forever, the plane burst out of the storm and into glaring sunlight, making an abrupt descent into Phoenix. Everyone filed off the plane and onto the tarmac like zombies.

Since I had an hour to kill, and had almost died, I found the closest bar right away. Gulping down two shots of vodka in quick succession, I noticed the woman on the stool next to me staring...*I'm a fucking wreck*. She looked like a Casino Trash Bingo Lady from Laughlin who'd been a stripper in her youth, with her fried blonde hair and sun-damaged skin covered in harsh, cheap make up.

"Been there, done that, got the T-shirt", she said with a kind, knowing expression crossing her weathered face.

"Your drinks are on me!" she stated firmly, ordering me another shot.

I don't really remember the flight back to LA, or for that matter, getting home. Immediately I called Prescott and learned that Pa had been transferred to The Yavapai County Detention Facility. Googling the number, I called, waiting through a series of automated prompts and recordings before I got a human being. At first, the CO wouldn't let me talk to him or leave a message, explaining that inmates couldn't receive them unless there was a Verified Emergency Situation. After I called back six or seven times in quick succession pretending to be a pregnant spouse, in exasperation, the guy finally said he'd give Pa the message and allow him to place a collect call to me.

Half an hour later, I gladly accepted the charges, rejoicing in hearing James' voice. He sounded good in spite of everything he'd been through: getting shackled with the "4-piece", the cuffs and chain arrangement usually reserved for serial killers, while sitting in the back of a squad car and then on a bench in Prescott waiting to get processed. He'd gone to jail in ancient, shredded jeans and a T-shirt emblazoned with a ventriloquist dummy that had a bloody Manson X on its forehead and "Puppet Terror" in drippy horror movie letters. He didn't have a cent on him and was barefoot, so he was booked as an "indigent". He still hadn't found out why he was being held or when he'd be released, but he sounded good. I promised to wire cash to be put into his commissary account and we phone-kissed. The call ended far too quickly but reassured that my lover wasn't being mistreated; I slept peacefully for just over twenty-four hours.

The next couple of days were filled with calls to his mother (who, not surprisingly, was cautious and extremely suspicious each time we spoke) and cyber-stalking the Yavapai County Detention Center, to the point that I knew how many employees the place had and all about the new prison-wide plumbing system that was in the midst of being installed.

In a couple more days, Pa finally discovered why he was being detained. It turned out that a court summons had erroneously been sent to an address that he hadn't lived at for *years*. Eventually it turned into a bench warrant, and the recent passing of the Patriot

Act had qualified any *fugitives from justice* to be extradited back to the state they'd fled for trial and/or punishment. So, Pa was held in custody in Arizona until New Mexico sent for his transport, which would land him in the Metropolitan Detention Center in Albuquerque until his trial. We'd *definitely* need a criminal lawyer to unravel this mess, even though it stemmed from a clerical error.

I was at an absolute loss at how to find a competent attorney in another state. There were dozens of them listed but trying to actually reach one on the phone was impossible. Either the lawyers would be "busy" and I'd be forced speak to a clueless paralegal who didn't understand the situation and apparently never left a message, or it was suggested that I come to New Mexico for a consultation, yeah, *right!* And then I remembered Mr. V.

I'd known Mr. V for years, he'd gone to school with one of my sisters. Somehow during a boozy party at her place, Mr. V had pegged me as a libertine and pulled me aside to confidentially ask me for sexual advice regarding his current girlfriend. Evidently, I counseled him quite well, because he began calling every few months to ask my take on getting a girl to role-play or how to introduce light bondage into a relationship. These calls became regular... like, every time he had a date (and he was dating a *lot*) but they were clean and clinical as opposed to kinky; I didn't feel creeped out at all. I *was* starting to feel like an unpaid sex therapist though. When he called for the third time in one week, wondering about coercing his latest fling into getting spanked, I'd joked that he would have to repay me someday. Since Mr. V was a former state senator who was currently a lawyer...*that time was now.*

As luck would have it, Mr. V was happy to reciprocate, hooking me up with a man who was supposed to be the best criminal defense attorney in the entire Southwest; he even wrote a personal letter of recommendation. The lawyer took the case, but the court date wouldn't be set until Pa was extradited back to New Mexico.

Meantime, James seemed to be having a fine time in the Detention Center, as detailed in his many letters to me. Along with heartfelt passages about how much he missed me, he wrote descriptions of day-to-day prison life. Apparently, because I was still calling the prison constantly to check on his status, I'd become something of a *celebrity* among the correctional officers. During the Lights Out rounds, while dragging a baton along the metal bars, one of them had even taken to clandestinely whispering out of the side of his mouth, "Hey! your wife called again!"

James' correspondence described all the various inmate cliques: the Mexicans who'd lift weights by attaching plastic trash bags full of water to each side of a broomstick, the trannies who offered haircuts to other inmates from their cell-salons, the Meth freaks and the White Power guys. He wrote about the shitty food, and the people who served it. The prison had separate buildings for men and women in the same compound, and the trustees serving the food worked both sides. For a price, they'd smuggle foil wrapped notes that were hidden under the lid of the plastic meal containers back and forth between lovers being held in different cellblocks. One letter of Pa's included pencil rubbings of the tweaker graffiti carved into the metal benches, another was written from the viewpoint of an ET who'd somehow been incarcerated.

Through the grapevine, he learned that many of the inmates believed Yavapai County was shaped like a Pentagram, and that the Sheriff's office was the very tip of the star. Then there was The Truth Hurts Incident. The only channel the big screen television in the common room ever played was MTV, all day and night. Pa just happened to be watching when my video made its debut. All the convicts were crowded around the TV, whistling and catcalling at the hip-hop hotties shaking their booties. When I swirled onto the screen in my sparkly blue and gold belly dance costume and veils, undulating in a "private dance" for Dr. Dre, Pa proudly announced to everyone that I was his girlfriend. Of course, they all thought he was joking!

He'd also become the star of a true Big House rags-to-riches story. Because of his artistic talent, he was now rolling in cigarettes, candy bars, Hostess Cakes, postage stamps and Swiss Miss drink packets…. all paid to him gladly by his fellow inmates. He was doing a roaring business drawing birthday and greeting cards to send to their mothers, wives and baby-mamas. His work was composed of intricate pencil drawings decorated with cherubs, hearts and roses colored in vivid yellows, and reds and greens, using uncooked Jell-O mix as paint. He even designed a tattoo of a raging bull for somebody, and watched it get inked into the guy's skin by hand. I could practically see the headlines: *Jailhouse Indigent Makes Good!*

On the last day it was possible to extradite James from Yavapai County to the Metropolitan Detention Center in Albuquerque, the New Mexico officers showed up. They'd flown over in a Cessna to bring James back to wait for his trial. Green-faced, one of the cops was so sick and terrified in the tiny plane that Pa wound up holding his hand the entire way.

The jail there was vastly different than in Arizona, Pa was put into General Population, which was basically a huge cage full of crazy people. In comparison, the Yavapai County Detention center had been a cakewalk. He kept a low profile as he waited for another two weeks for his day in court.

Apparently, Mr. V had done an absolutely bang-up job of finding an attorney. Though the lawyer was hideously expensive, he was, *for real*, the best criminal defense attorney in the state. He was also the presiding judge's golf buddy and had been a mentor to the prosecuting lawyer when he'd been in law school!

A few days after the trial, James returned to Hollywood in his rattletrap pickup truck. He hugged me long and tight, and we kissed for eons.

"I brought you a present from jail!", he said jubilantly, handing me a grocery bag and a tattered newspaper clipping.

Some guys learn how to crack safes or become bookies when they're on the inside; others kill their fellow inmates with shanks made from a toothbrush. But Pa had been going through magazines in Albuquerque, looking for *recipes*. The one he handed me was for Southern Fried chicken, written by Martha Stewart…a good two years before she herself was incarcerated.

"I'm starving," Pa said, getting out a frying pan.

"Let's try this!"

As I handed him the contents of the grocery bag, he squeezed me and sighed regretfully,

"You know, when we were in Kingman, and the gas pump said $9.11? I didn't think that was a good sign, and I wanted to stay there at the motel…but I didn't tell you because I thought you'd think I was crazy!"

FULL HOUSE

I spent most of 2007 and 2008 dancing in *The Sensuous Woman*, comedian Margaret Cho's boundary pushing, gender-bending burlesque and variety show. The production melded Margaret's outrageous standup up comedy with classic and surreal post-modern striptease plus a slew of hilarious song-and-dance numbers. "Sen-Wo", as we affectionately called it in homage to J-Lo, originally started as a one-off benefit show at the historic Los Angeles nightclub El Cid. It immediately sold out and we were asked to do a residency there, which lasted several months. That led to dates in San Francisco and an appearance on Fire Island, New York's famed LGBTQ vacation enclave. Eventually a tour was booked, which included a week in Chicago and a nine-week Off Broadway run in New York City.

The show was outrageously wild by *anyone's* standards. Margaret stripped languorously to classical opera until she was totally nude before parting her huge, feathered fans to reveal a disturbingly realistic flaccid penis. Transgender comedian Ian Harvie's set focused on his misadventures trying to get a bag of dildos through the TSA security checkpoint at an airport. Selene Luna, a 3'10" comedian and burlesque dancer known as "The Pocket Venus", rode onstage in a vintage baby carriage before toddling around stripping out of a christening gown and frilly bonnet. Liam Sullivan performed his hit song *Shoes* as his teenage nerd-drag alter ego Kelly; queen-sized burlesque legend Dirty Martini did "The Patriot

Act", which concluded with her pulling an endless string of dollar bills out of her ass. Mustachioed dancer Ryan Heffington rampaged through Michael Jackson's *Dirty Diana* dressed in acid-washed 1980s denim and a miniscule G-string, doing splits in over-the-knee platform boots before climbing over the chairs to assault audience members with uber-raunchy lap dances. In comparison, my *Wizard Of Oz* act as a slutty, stripping Dorothy Gale who gets molested by a raunchy Flying Monkey appeared *tame*.

All prurient lunacy aside, the entire cast was always just a little stunned at the show's popularity, who would've *ever* thought that that an audience made up of about ninety-five percent queer men would flock to a show which primarily featured women twirling tasseled pasties?

In order to up the ante even further, it was decided that for the tour, we'd add in a couple of Busby Berkeley type group numbers for the opening and grand finale. We moved into another residency, this time at the Los Angeles LGBT Center's Renberg Theater in Hollywood to woodshed the new, improved show before taking it on the road. We rehearsed at the Center through most of June and July, before finally moving into the theater itself for our dress and technical rehearsals plus a couple of teaser shows. The whole cast was pleased with the venue; in addition to state-of-the-art sound and lights, the Renberg featured modern plush chairs, which reclined for optimal audience comfort.

During our first tech rehearsal, my Flying Monkey Ian and I decided to go out into the middle of the house to see what the stage looked like from the audience. Since it's always difficult to know what the stage lighting looks like when you're actually standing *under* it, we decided to take photos for reference. As we whipped out our smart phones, Margaret was onstage going through her "Chairman Meow" burlesque number. She was in mid-striptease, peeling off a vintage Chinese Army uniform, her twin braids peeking out from under her Mao hat.

"Hey, look at this," Ian cried, perturbed, brandishing his phone under my nose,

"It looks like it's *snowing* in here!"

The photo he'd taken captured the whole theater as well as the stage, and the entire image was chock full of orbs. Some people think that orbs, the white or translucent spheres that appear as anomalies on photos, are merely dust particles on the camera lens, but others believe they're a visual manifestation of spirits. Many are convinced that when orbs show up on film, it's a sign that angels are nearby.

As Ian aggressively dusted off his phone screen and camera lens, I snapped a comparison photo on my phone; the resulting picture was exactly the same as his.

Ian cocked his head, arched an eyebrow and asked,

"Do you think these are *orbs*?"

We immediately both wondered out loud about the possibility of the Renberg being haunted, as several theaters are reputed to be. In fact, historically, so *many* theaters are alleged to be inhabited by ghosts that for the past decade, the famed New York Theater publication *Playbill* actually tracks, and publishes, sightings of apparitions and other reports of paranormal activity in the annual *Broadway Yearbook*. After a "spirited" discussion, we both decided that since the Renberg Theater was built quite recently, it probably *wasn't* haunted after all.

Just then, the venue's director Jon Imperato came up to us, asking if we were pleased with the theater. We assured him we were, and making small talk, Ian asked how many people the theater held. Jon's answer stunned us into silence.

"We hold five hundred", he said, making a sweeping gesture before adding,

"Each seat in here is dedicated to the memory someone who died of HIV or AIDS-related complications. There's a plaque on the back of *every chair*."

As Jon walked off to check the box office, Ian and I looked around. Indeed, every damn chair in the place had a plaque on it, with the name, birth and death dates of the individual it honored.

Glancing down at our phones to view the orb-filled photos once more, Ian and I locked eyes.

Wrinkling his forehead as he surveyed the theater, Ian nodded a few times as though he was processing his thoughts, before exhaling slowly and saying enthusiastically,

"Well... I sure hope all you guys enjoy the show!"

LOST IN THE HAUNTED FOREST

Everyone knows Halloween is big business. In California alone, there are more than 25 large scale haunted houses and seasonal attractions; that's not even counting corporate giants like Disneyland, Universal Studios and Knott's Scary Farm. So when my witchy sister and ghost hunting partner Crystal Ravenwolf and I were contacted about doing a paranormal investigation at Hobbs Grove, one of the top, privately-owned Halloween Haunts on the West Coast, we jumped at the chance.

Located in the heart of California's San Joaquin Valley near the rural hamlet of Sanger, the former walnut plantation has thrown its creaky doors open as a spooky theme park every October for nearly two decades. In 2015, their "Spokes Ghoul" Maverick Cadaverick reached out to us because the hundred or so members of the cast and crew were alarmed at the *real* paranormal activity on the property. Several had actually quit their jobs, refusing to return.

Maverick stated that many of the staff and seasonal cast had already been experiencing true paranormal phenomena for years, but ever since an autopsy table and a load of vintage stretchers were acquired from Wolfe Manor in nearby Clovis, the activity had escalated exponentially. A tuberculosis sanitarium in the 1930s, in the following decades, rumors of gross negligence and patient abuse at Wolfe Manor circulated throughout the Central Valley. Extremely haunted and known for being a spirit hot spot, Wolfe

Manor had become a beacon for psychics, mediums and paranormal investigators, and has been featured on the television shows *Ghost Hunters* and *Ghost Adventures*. Maverick was concerned that the medical items were filled with residual negative energy. There was also the matter of the recently acquired coffin; it had been used to transport a body from Mexico to the USA. Evidently, nobody working at Hobbs dared to go anywhere near it, and everyone declined to say why.

Maverick also sent an email with several pages worth of the employee reports detailing apparition sightings, odd sounds, cold spots, disembodied speaking and singing voices and generally unexplained anomalies, stuff like moving furniture and small, everyday objects disappearing, never to be seen again.

Hobbs Grove features three distinct attractions: The Haunted Forest, a Haunted Hayride and a Haunted House built inside a large barn. We wanted to explore *all* of it, especially after reading the worker's reports, which were chilling.

On the first night of his job in the forest, one actor was so entranced by the hologram he saw, a legless head and torso of a man floating in the air wearing a 1930s suit, that at the end of his shift, the actor marveled out loud about the sophisticated holographic technology to his co-workers. After some uncomfortable glances exchanged by the rest of the large crew, someone finally pointed out that Hobbs Grove didn't have *any* holograms!

Then there was the time an employee on the Hayride went to one of the park's trailers to get firewood and was met with a rumbling low growl, even though there were no dogs, coyotes, or even humans in sight. Another worker reported seeing a set disembodied of legs and feet running across the rafters in the barn, claiming that

that'd actually heard the apparition's footsteps. Still a third noticed a uniformed security guard enter the room where he was working. The guard, who'd appeared to be human at first, slowly turned transparent before disappearing through a solid wall.

And there was also the legendary evening a week before Halloween when Hobbs was at full capacity and all operations ground to a complete halt because of "legit" supernatural activity. Dozens of veteran performers in the Haunted Forest had witnessed a large, industrial sized wooden cable spool, the type used for telephone wires, rolling through the woods *by itself*. The actors, many of whom had been working there for years, were so freaked out they immediately evacuated their posts en masse. The entire park, which was full of hundreds of customers had to be shut down while the actors, who all steadfastly refused to return to the forest, were finally reassigned and a new crew was sent to the woods.

Excited to investigate this highly active area, Crystal and I set our ghost hunt for the first weekend in August. On the first night, we invited veteran paranormal investigators Jan Acosta and Keri Foss-Jastztremski along to come with us. Highly respected in the paranormal community, the mother and daughter team are known for their knowledge, site research, no-nonsense investigative style and meticulous evidence collection. Affectionately known as "Mom", Jan has mentored several generations of ghost hunters since the 1970s. On Saturday, Crystal and I were scheduled to teach Paranormal Investigation 101 at a metaphysical store called The Cosmic Corral; we'd be taking the students on a field trip to Hobbs that evening.

Each night of the investigation, we brought an arsenal of ghost hunting equipment, from traditional divining rods to state-of-the art high tech devices. We were armed with EVP (electronic voice phenomena) recorders, EMF detectors, which show changes in the electromagnetic field by lighting up; and a REM Pod, a device which emanates its own electromagnetic field through a miniature antenna. When the instrument's field is entered by an energy source, such as an entity, the REM Pod lights up. Mom also brought an Ovilus, a device with a thesaurus-like database of words programmed into it, contains thousands of different verbs, adjectives, nouns and adverbs that the spirits can use to communicate. The way an Ovilus works is that during an investigation, an intelligent spirit will make itself known in a way that modifies the environment. The Ovilus then converts these irregularities into the words contained in the machine. Maverick had also hired a professional videographer to film the investigations each night.

Both evenings were nothing short of *batshit,* in all our years of ghost hunting, Crystal and I agreed that the activity at Hobbs Grove probably topped even our several investigations aboard The RMS Queen Mary, reputed to be one of the most haunted places on earth.

On the first night we were drawn to the barn, a large structure that included the green room for the Grove's performers, and the location where many employees heard footsteps coming from the loft. The moment we entered, we heard odd bumping noises and felt the temperature drop. The sounds were so constant we turned on our equipment right away, while Maverick texted the employees who were onsite, threatening to fire them if they were playing practical jokes.

They were not.

Originally, Keri was unsure if a Halloween attraction could honestly be haunted, but once all the devices went off the charts, she quickly changed her mind, saying,

"I thought to myself, 'We're investigating a Halloween park to see if it's *haunted*? Who'd believe this one?' But wow... the activity here is just crazy!"

Our Rem pod lit up like a Christmas tree while Keri's divining rods swung to and fro, answering yes/no questions that were confirmed by everything a spirit named Robert said through the Ovilus. While Maverick and another employee watched in amazement, we all carried on a conversation for about ten minutes, until Robert suddenly stopped talking.

The room remained chilly, and the REM pod was shining, so we knew he was still there. We tried to cajole Robert back into the conversation, but he was silent, so we started packing up to move to another location. As Keri put her rods away, I turned off the REM pod, putting it back into the bag, but suddenly, it was visible through the fabric; it had lit up again...by itself.

Rolling her eyes, Mom chided, "You *need* to turn that off!"

Scooping the device out of the bag, I held it up showing her that the switch was indeed turned to off. Raising and eyebrow, Mom said it must be defective. I removed the batteries in front of everyone, but the lights on the device stayed on. It didn't stop glowing until hours later, well after we returned home.

Since we could all feel that Robert was still with us, and the cold spots and REM pod seemed to confirm it, Crystal resorted to a light-hearted last-ditch effort to get him to speak again.

Tossing her hair and arching her back, she joked in a seductive voice,

"What's the matter, don't you wanna talk to a couple of hot chicks?"

The Ovilus immediately sprang into action, its robotic voice declaring emphatically,

"MOM'S HOTTER!"

After a moment of disbelief, Mom did a victory dance, arms upraised, howling "Thass right…thass right!" as everyone in the room laughed so hard, we were literally crying.

It soon became apparent that Robert's comedic *tour de force* was his last communication, so we decided to investigate the Haunted House.

Constructed with a maze-like interior, the Haunted House features all sorts of gory scenes and a gigantic room packed from floor to ceiling with legions of dirty, uber-creepy baby dolls, many missing glassy eyes, hair or limbs. It is widely acknowledged among parapsychologists that dolls make terrific hiding places for spirits, for whatever reason, possibly the human form, entities are attracted to them. Though the doll room was heavy with energy, we didn't get as many hits as we expected, but there was so much activity around the stretchers from Wolfe Manor that with an involuntary shiver, Mom urged Maverick,

"You need to get rid of those things *now*!"

Moving outside, we encountered an extremely negative entity that was hanging around a cottage near the barn.

"Over the years, I've found that if human spirits were hateful, spiteful, rude, abusive drunks or…any other "expletives" while they were alive, they're the same in death", Keri said, continuing,

"Like George, that chauvinist pig spirit who tried to give Crystal attitude. He showed his true colors, belittling and cussing at her. Crystal told him off and had quite an interesting argument with him for a while…it was only after she stood her ground did he back off!"

Around 1:00am, we all called it a night because we had to be up early to teach our workshop. As the class concluded, we reminded the group that during the course of a ghost hunt, there's often a whole lot of dead time, pun very much intended, and often, the spirits just don't want to come out and play. That night, we were wrong.

Even with a large group, things got *insane* almost from the moment we set foot on the property. The videographer Maverick hired joined us to document the entire hunt. Initially, Dude Bro claimed in an offhand way that he didn't believe in ghosts, and though he was documenting everything professionally, it was abundantly clear that he thought the whole thing was childish and silly.

As the sun set, we trudged into the forest with Maverick in the lead, holding an antique glass gas lantern. Our first stop was the "Redneck Camp" on the Haunted Hayride route, a collection of five hideously trashed vintage trailers. Since it was the location where an employee reported the growling sounds, we figured it was a great place to start. The students pulled out their equipment, and everyone got hits immediately. Once again, I set up the REM pod and right away, it lit up with so many colors, it resembled the dance floor in *Saturday Night Fever*. As various investigational devices were activated and Crystal busted out her divining rods, I asked the spirits,

"How do you guys like being here, living right in the middle of a Halloween Haunt?"

I'd barely finished my sentence when the Ovilus chirped,

"It's *perfect!*"

Many of the students had Spirit Boxes, and all of them were talking simultaneously. Crystal turned to make sure the videographer was getting all the activity on film, and he was nowhere to be found... until she spotted him far down the path, *running away!*

Sprinting after him, she finally caught up. White as an old school trick-or-treating Sheet Ghost, he told her breathlessly that the moment we got to the trailers, he'd felt as though someone had dumped a bucket of ice water down his back.

"I'm *outta* here," he cried in a falsetto panic, slinging the camera bag over his shoulder and sprinting towards the parking lot,

"I didn't sign up for this shit...I can't *do* this!"

Just another sceptic turned True Believer.

We went on to investigate the Haunted Forest, stopping numerous times, to set up for EVPS and Ovilus sessions, all of which were documented by our own photographer, who fortunately hadn't yet lost it from all the paranormal activity. Crystal and a few others spotted a large black Shadow Person darting behind a tree; everyone got more hits at the various sites, which were a maze of spooky cottages and junked automobiles, all overgrown with tangled wild vines.

One of the many spirits we communicated with was a little girl; later, Maverick confirmed that many employees had reported seeing a small female child dressed in 1920s clothes roaming the property or had heard children laughing when none were present.

Both investigations at Hobbs Grove were so active, that Mom, swooning like a teenager in the throes of a crush said dreamily,

"The creep factor at Hobbs Grove was so overwhelming, I don't think a Hollywood script could have written *that* scenario!"

THE UNINVITED GUEST

I awoke suddenly with a sharp gasp, like a heroine in a 1960s Hammer Films horror movie. I was more surprised than scared, but the adrenalin flooding my system told me I was on high alert. Remaining still, I listened for suspicious sounds until I was satisfied that no one was inside the house. Then I noticed the circle of mist on my ceiling. It was a perfect ring, about a foot and a half in diameter, glowing the jarring lime green of radiator fluid like a neon halo. It revolved in such a lazy counterclockwise orbit that I wasn't even sure it was actually moving.

Fully conscious and completely sober, I'm also ridiculously blind. My eyes didn't stray from the circling mist as I groped for my glasses on the bedside table, certain it was an optical illusion caused by the darkness and my bad eyesight. Sliding my specs on, the radium-like glow became crisp and intensified. It occurred to me that the misty circle was probably emanating from the little operation light on my smoke detector, mounted on the wall behind my bed. I twisted around to check; the light was on all right, but it was red, not pale green.

Convinced I was experiencing a lucid dream, I clambered out of bed in order to wake myself fully. I entered the bathroom, flicking on the light switch. I peed, wiped, flushed the toilet, washed my hands, dried them, and applied some lotion. Satisfied that I had performed enough mundane actions to prove that I was truly awake, I turned off the bathroom light, padding the down the hall to my bedroom.

Tossing my glasses carelessly onto the bedside table, I crawled back into bed without looking at the ceiling. Deliberately keeping my eyes closed, I pulled the comforter up all cozy under my chin.

An internal debate started.

I felt like a cartoon character with a devil on one shoulder and an angel on the other as a two-way conversation began inside my head.

So, are you really going to go to sleep without checking to see if that thing is still on the ceiling?

Yeah... it'll be ok.

The First Voice paused for a moment in an attempt to comprehend the stupidity of the Second Voice's answer before snapping,

Are you fucking high?

With that, my eyes fluttered open tentatively, and I realized two things simultaneously: that the mist was indeed still there, and its very presence was a confirmation that I hadn't in fact, been dreaming. With more than a passing feeling of discomfort, I also understood that in order to have gotten back into bed completely willing to *not* check on the mist, that it somehow must've been hypnotizing me into compliance. Whatever this was, it was real...and it was now brighter, solidifying and definitely moving faster. As I watched the revolutions become more rapid, I tried to think practically and stuff down the dread that was rising up in my chest.

The First Voice suggested,

You should say The Lord's Prayer.

The Second Voice replied with disdain,

Someone's seen waaaay too many horror movies!

Ignoring the Second Voice, I telepathically communicated to the first Voice,

"Should I actually say it or is it ok to just think it?"

There's no one else here, the First Voice answered, *either way is fine.*

Dutifully, I recited out loud,

"Dearly Beloved…"

The Second Voice cut me off immediately:

You idiot, that's not The Lord's Prayer, who doesn't know the fucking Lord's Prayer? That's for a funeral or a wedding or something…get it together!

Seriously, what kind of a lame-ass was I? I hadn't really been raised with religion but, pun intended, God knows how many times I'd seen *The Exorcist,* and I certainly listened to Siouxsie And The Banshee's 1979 punk version of The Lord's Prayer enough to have the entire thing memorized. I wracked my brains, groping for the correct words before I began tentatively,

"Our Father who art in Heaven, hallowed by thy name…"

The vapor pulsed on the ceiling, blinking rhythmically while it spun, as though it was transmitting a code. True panic made the back of my neck tingle as I furtively wondered if I should ask it to leave.

Before the First or Second voice even had a chance to chime in with their opinions, my real voice took on a forceful tone that wasn't my own as I commanded loudly:

"IN THE NAME OF JESUS CHRIST, YOU NEED TO LEAVE NOW!"

The words were barely out of my mouth when an intense pitch-black dot appeared in the center of the mist, accompanied by a quick pressure drop in my ear canals, as though I was in a plane that was losing altitude quickly. Suddenly, like stop motion animation, the black dot widened with a roaring sound, and as it did, the green mist grew with it, swirling precariously. The mist circle suddenly split in two, both halves leaving the ceiling and shooting down towards the bed, encircling it. Just as rapidly, they launched upwards roaring through the hole, before disappearing inside it. The hole then sealed itself shut with a deafening crack.

I bolted upright, my hair on end, my entire body covered in goose bumps. Slapping the bedroom light on as I leapt out of bed, I crashed through the hall, knocking a couple framed photos off the wall. I turned on the bathroom light, the lamp and overhead fixture in the in the living room, and both kitchen lights. Pacing like a lunatic, I switched on the television, the radio, and my computer. The clock said 3:33 which is reputed to be The Witching Hour; as soon as I saw it, I began to cry. It was way too early to call anyone, and even if I did, *what the hell was I going to say?* Anyone who knew me would only ask if I'd started doing drugs again.

I had no clue what had just happened to me, but I didn't feel comfortable with it…at all. I stayed up listening to *Coast To Coast* on the radio followed by a drive time local news program, chain smoking and doing busy work that I never *normally* would do, like reorganizing my bookshelves and dusting. When it seemed a decent hour, I went out and got sage and Palo Santo, smudging my entire place with the windows flung open before salting the doors and windowsills.

A month or so later, a neighbor who lived in the front apartment of our hundred-year-old residence asked if I thought it was haunted. He said that the night before, he'd heard footsteps on the roof. I asked him if he was sure it wasn't raccoons, and he told me he'd gone out with a flashlight and checked; there were no raccoons in sight.

We barely knew each other, but after sizing him up for a moment, I decided he seemed like he'd be able handle my story without getting too freaked out. I told him everything. There was an awfully pause before he asked,

"Why didn't you call me?"

"Oh, sure," I said, trying as hard as I could not to roll my eyes,

"Like I was really gonna call you in the middle of the night to tell you that a *portal* opened up on my ceiling?"

"I guess not," he said sincerely, "But if it happens again, please call me!"

A week after we had that conversation, it *did* happen again…but this time I was prepared. The mist manifested sharp, dense and much larger this time. It had barbs and points sticking out of it like a really badly done late 1980s Tribal tattoo. I'd been on the verge of drifting off when it appeared, so it was a lot less disorienting than being awakened from REM sleep. Narrowing my eyes as I stared directly at it, I addressed it loudly, with the psychotic bravado of Robert De Niro as Travis Bickel in *Taxi Driver*:

"You talkin' to *me?*"

This time I bypassed the First Voice, The Second Voice and The Lord's Prayer, roaring like a battle cry:

"IN THE NAME OF JESUS CHRIST YOU HAVE TO LEAVE RIGHT NOW!"

And it did.

The portal sealed itself back up and the pressure normalized in my ears. Before I rolled over and went to sleep, I saw that the clock once again said 3:33. The next day, my neighbor didn't mention hearing me yelling, and the mist never came back.

BELLE, BOOK, AND CANDLE

Ever since I was kid, I'd been obsessed with the classic 1958 film *Bell, Book And Candle*, starring Kim Novak as a Gillian Holroyd, a gorgeous, blonde beatnik sorceress living in Manhattan. Along with her feline familiar Pyewacket and to-die-for wardrobe, Gillian also practiced love magick on her handsome neighbor, played by James Stuart. She brings him to The Zodiac Club, a cool underground speakeasy for witches in Greenwich Village. As a little girl, I'd watch that movie whenever it came on television, dreaming of being a glamorous New York City witch sashaying around The Zodiac Club.

More than fifty years later, I dreamed of The Zodiac club again, but it wasn't exactly the same as in the film, it was even cooler. There were stunning women dancing onstage as witches, devils, goddesses, bats and cats. Some looked straight up Goth or fetish-adjacent; others were retro beauties with luxurious costumes covered in thousands of sparkling rhinestones. Mounted on the walls of the (new, improved) dreamland version of The Zodiac Club were three large red neon signs, their fancy, Mid Century Atomic Age script emitting a soft glow. One simply said *Burlesque,* the second was *Sub Rosa*, Latin for "under the rose" referring to secrecy, mystery and ritual. The last sign read *Belle Book And Candle* with an "e" added onto the word belle transforming it into the feminine French word for "beautiful".

Waking from this wonderfully sexy vision, my only takeaway was that I needed to start a dark burlesque show... immediately. I could see it clearly: the production would be all occult themed, with the acts encompassing everything from myths and legends to *sexified* Divine Feminine archetypes. There had to be psychics and an on-stage ritual. Logistically, a raised stage was mandatory so that the dancers didn't have to perform among the crowd; there also needed to be a quiet place for the psychics to do readings. The only hitch I anticipated was that since I hadn't been back home in Los Angeles for any significant amount of time due to my touring dance schedule, I was no longer familiar with the layouts, or the talent bookers of potential venues.

As fate would have it, the doors flew open immediately; it was just a matter of saying yes to the universe and crossing each threshold.

Days later, I got a call from a girl named Shana. She was a new burlesque gal who wanted to level up her dance game; someone had referred her to me for private lessons. As opposed to using my real name, she used my stage moniker Princess Farhana. Her name was more common than mine, so it took us a little bit to figure out that we already knew each other from the witchy shop The Green Man Store.

When Shana came into my studio, the act she wanted to work on was a hot chair number she'd named "Voodoo Housewife". She already had a lot of it choreographed and with her arresting neon pink hair and multiple tattoos, it was clear that both her dance persona and *civilian* aesthetic was identical to mine. Though she'd been doing burlesque for under a year, I was seriously impressed. She had strong presence and took direction like a seasoned performer. We worked together a while longer and each time she was miles beyond most typical students in terms of technique, stage presence and costuming.

We started bonding hard and she asked me to perform at her birthday party. The venue was a dive bar; though there was no dressing room, at least it had a stage. I did my two numbers, socialized a bit, and then I realized there were psychics; a couple of readers from The Green Man Store were slinging cards at the tables in the corner...just like in my dream.

Waiting a day for Shana's birthday hangover to subside, I called her, described the dream and asked if she'd co-produce the new show with me; the only caveat was it had to be in a beautiful venue with a raised stage. She agreed immediately; we settled on the name *Belle, Book And Candle*. Getting the dancers and psychics wouldn't be a problem, we both had wide social circles and I knew almost everyone who was *anyone* in the burlesque world; alluring, internationally known performers. But we needed to find the perfect home for our witchy show. My number one choice was El Cid, a historic venue located on Sunset Boulevard. It was a landmark and totally Old Hollywood. The vintage neon sign was at street level, but down a steep flight of uneven brick steps, there was a fantastically overgrown tropical garden framing a gigantic patio...which would be the perfect place for psychics. The stage was raised, had decent lighting and a curtain; there were private dressing rooms. The bonus was that it was haunted, I knew that for a fact because I'd been performing there for almost thirty years. Some of the staff even refused to stay after Last Call due to all the paranormal activity. Over the decades, El Cid been everything from a soundstage for silent films to a dinner theater featuring Flamenco dancers. In the 1930s, when it was known as The Jail Café, it was the hottest ticket in town, complete with iron bars on the windows and wardens at the door. The waiters wore striped prison uniforms to serve famous movie stars dinner and cocktails in battered tin cups and plates. Sadly, in the years I'd been touring, I'd heard the club had gone pretty far south: apparently, there weren't decent shows anymore and the place was falling into dire disrepair.

Shana and I went out on the town a few times each week for the sole purpose of finding the perfect venue. It seemed like every club we went to had a great stage but lacked a place for the psychics, or it was multi-room club, but didn't have a stage and dressing rooms. I kept thinking fondly of El Cid, but it didn't seem tenable. We started to get disheartened, thinking we'd need to compromise.

One day I woke up, and The Voice in my head kept saying: *Call Lina, she can help you with the show!*

I'd known Lina Lecaro from the 1980s, when I was fully immersed in the wild LA rock scene. She was an up-and-coming baby writer and I thought she was a delightful person with a lot of talent, drive and promise. Years later, she told me that I'd inspired her, and I got all warm and fuzzy. She'd gone on to become an author, a newspaper editor and a multi-talented music maven: she was highly respected and knew everyone in Hollywood.

My clairaudience was relentless: it didn't stop, insistently urging me to call her all day long. Ultimately, I knew I *needed* to, even though we hadn't seen each other in a few year years. Scrolling through my contacts, I found her number, which I hoped was still good, and left a voice message asking for her input on an idea I had. Minutes later, the phone rang. After playing catch-up, Lina asked what I wanted to run by her, so I told her all about the show.

"Wow! That sounds *fantastic*!" she replied enthusiastically,

"Where are you thinking of doing it?"

"Well, I kinda hoped *you* could help me with that..."

Since I certainly wasn't about to tell her that a disembodied paranormal voice was pestering me to call her, I listed every place Shana and I had checked out, adding that there a particular venue I had in mind, and wanted to know what she thought.

"What club is that?' she asked.

When I said El Cid, the phone went absolutely silent. For a second, it seemed we'd been disconnected; but then I thought Lina was being quiet because it was such an awful idea.

Finally, in a confidential, almost suspicious tone, Lina asked,

"Did someone tell you I started booking El Cid last night?"

My knee-jerk reaction was yelling "WHAT!?" so hard, it seemed entirely possible that my outburst had ruptured her eardrum.

Lina explained the venue had recently changed hands; the new owner had made a lot of improvements, with more to come. She offered us a Wednesday night for the show, but it was only two weeks away. I knew Shana and I could pull off the entire production– booking and promoting it, within two weeks, but I had a counteroffer. We'd take the night Lina had in mind, but *only* if Belle, Book And Candle could have the third Witchy Wednesday of every month for the summer, because Shana and I believed we could turn it into A Thing. Initially, Lina said she wasn't sure the owner would go for it…but he did.

Even before the dancers were booked, I did the astrology, numerology and Tarot for the date of our first show, which was set for May17, 2017. As it happened, Belle Book And Candle was a Taurus: an ambitious, determined Earth sign. Ruled by the planet Venus, any Taurus, *but especially our show,* would be all about beauty, love, artistry and sensuality. The numerology of the opening show was a 6, representing harmony and partnerships; creating a nurturing, family style environment. The Tarot card was The Lovers: all about relationships, partnerships, bonding and making strong decisions. In short, Shana and I were in the process of creating a show that, stunning witchy strippers aside, had a wonderful metaphysical vibe.

Two weeks later, Belle, Book And Candle had a sold-out debut. The next show, which (thanks, universe!) just happened to be on the exact day of Summer Solstice, also sold out. In that first year, the show also hit directly on Autumn Equinox *and* every New Moon or Dark Moon. It was uncanny-people were asking us how far in advance we'd booked the shows in order for them to coincide with pagan *sabbats* and the phases of the Moon!

Though it was obvious to others before it was to Shana and me, Belle, Book And Candle had become *the* monthly gathering place for magical practitioners, pagans, burlesque fans and basically, weirdos of all stripes. Audience members, the dancers, psychics and vendors alike all constantly commented on how comfortable they felt in the congenial, accepting atmosphere we'd created, as well as the diversity of the show. Our goal was to have an event where *everyone* was welcome and felt safe and seen. Our performers were of every possible ethnicity, body type, age and gender identity. Each time we heard somebody alluding to or enforcing our idea, Shana and I would almost start crying: it was so wonderful to see our vision come true. Wait, instead of vision, make that the magickal dream we manifested into reality through a glorious string of synchronicities.

** ** **

At the time of this writing the show has been running for five years.

SEND IN THE CLOUDS

My first client of the day sauntered into my reading room reeking of Movie Biz Exec: freshly clipped silver hair, a salon tan, distressed jeans that were obviously purchased that way and expensive-but-understated Italian loafers.

Somehow, I'd made it to my late fifties without ever working at a metaphysical shop. I'd done countless readings for my Tarot clients, plenty of private parties, psychic fairs and corporate events. Business was booming, but I needed to have a workspace that wasn't my home office. So when I was offered a job working as a psychic at my favorite witchy shop The Green Man Store, I jumped at the chance.

The Green Man is a magickal incense and herb scented oasis located in the middle of a "transitional" North Hollywood neighborhood, just outside the Arts District. Urban pagans from all over Southern California gathered for classes, group rituals, to buy spell supplies and get various types of readings and healings from the seven or so psychics on duty every day. The graffiti-marked side streets were sketchy, littered with discarded mattresses, tweakers pushing shopping carts piled high with trash, and what appeared to be the remnants of *Santeria* rituals casually tossed into weed-filled flower beds. In stark contrast, Warner Brothers and Universal Studios were just a few blocks away. I wasn't quite sure what to expect, but hoped my clientele would be more hipsters, producers and aspiring actors than street crazies… and then Mr. Entertainment Industry appeared.

My first client, not only of the day, but at The Greenman itself, took a seat, exchanging his designer sunglasses for readers. I asked his birthday while shuffling the deck as he discretely tucked a folded twenty-dollar tip under the large hunk of Malachite sitting on my table.

His reading showed prosperity, the need to make carefully calculated life choices, and a relationship with a person who didn't have closure on old emotional wounds, projecting them on him. He listened politely, nodding in affirmation as I spoke. After we'd gotten to the possible outcome, so called because the future is considered mutable due to the seeker's free will, I asked if he had any questions. He pointed to the Knight Of Wands and asked what it meant; I explained it again.

"I only know a little about Tarot," he said, "But I'm a *very* spiritual person."

"I'm sure you are," I replied, "otherwise you wouldn't be here!"

"Would you like to know what I do?' he asked, as though he couldn't wait to tell me.

"Of course," I answered, assuming he was going to say he meditated or was a Kundalini Yoga devotee. Perhaps he dabbled in Wicca or some other esoteric practice.

"You *really* want to know?" he enquired as though he was about to reveal a huge, wondrous surprise.

I studied him for a second: he didn't really seem the type for Satanism or Ceremonial Magic…but you never know; outward appearances can be deceiving. He leaned across the table, almost, but not quite, invading my personal space. His gaze was intense as his eyes locked on mine.

Without breaking visual contact, he spoke as though there was a period punctuating every word he said.

"I control the clouds on Oahu!"

This was so bizarre, not to mention super specific, I valiantly tried to keep a neutral look on my face as my brain practically screamed, *Use your acting skills!*

"Wow," I said enthusiastically, "What about the other islands, do you control their clouds too? Or only Oahu?"

He whipped the reading glasses off his face like a cheesy early '80s Television Star. It was the type of gesture Eric Estrada frequently used with his aviator cop shades on *CHiPs* so as to appear sincere while still emitting a sense of power and authority. Tilting the front legs of his chair off the floor, Mr. Entertainment Industry leaned back, cocking his head, raising his eyebrows and crossing his arms in what seemed to be an expansive, non-verbal way of saying *You're Welcome.*

"That's…so cool," I said, hoping I sounded sufficiently grateful for his unique meteorological service. I escorted him down the stairs and through the front door.

At the end of the shift, as all the psychics gathered to turn in their daily reading slips, I asked if they ever discussed their clients. When they assured me that they did, I dished on Mr. Entertainment Biz. Some stared in amazement, a few cracked up. To this day, some of us randomly text each other photos of clouds and it never fails to get a laugh.

TATTOO YOU

On New Year's Day 2019, I woke up in full Manifestation Mode. In three months I was turning sixty, and things were definitely going to change. There was no way I could endure a year that was as hectic as 2018 had been, *no way*. So with my cats as witnesses, I proclaimed out loud: *My resolution is to slow-roll through this year...and so it is!*

Later that afternoon, driving back from a New Year's brunch, my gay Forever Husband Greg pointed out a huge Psychic Reader And Advisor sign. Sticking my arm out the window and pointing like a toddler, I whined,

"I've wanted one of those my whole life...since I was twelve! *I need a psychic sign!*

When Greg told me that our mutual friend Marcella had just picked one up at a swap meet, I got so upset I that I literally had to pull over. Yanking the emergency break, I turned the ignition off and had a full-on meltdown, pounding on the steering wheel like a crazy person, hollering at the top of my lungs,

"That's *it!* I'm *changing* my New Year's Resolution right *now!* This is the year I get a goddamn psychic sign!"

The next morning, I woke up to so many text alerts that my first thought was that someone had died. Trying to think optimistically,

I hoped that maybe I'd just managed to sleep through a small earthquake. Grabbing my phone all bleary eyed and assuming the worst, I couldn't believe what I was seeing; *Am I still asleep? Is this a dream?*

There were six separate texts from my ex-boyfriend Jeff, and they were *all* photos of two different Reader And Advisor signs. Both were so amazing that they put the one I'd seen on the street to shame. The last message was the only one containing words. It said: *Do you want these?*

Staggering into the kitchen and slamming down a cup of day-old coffee in one gulp, I dialed Jeff's number. Without even saying hello, I started talking way too fast in an auctioneer style run-on sentence.

"Are the signs for sale? Where are they? Buy them immediately! I'll PayPal you…I'll Venmo you…I'll drive over and drop cash off! I don't care how much they are, wait, how much *are* they? No…I don't give a shit! You gotta get those signs, *I need them*!"

He laughed his signature long, slow chuckle before saying,

"Calm down, baby…I found them on the street in the trash! They're yours now."

Apparently, the universe was listening carefully, taking it literally when I changed my resolution. I got my beloved psychic signs, but 2019 turned out to be my busiest year ever. While I've always had a healthy, no, make that *zealous,* work ethic, in 2019 it reached a whole new level. I took an epic swan dive into the depths of workaholic depravity. I produced and danced in a number of shows, taught Tarot and dance workshops, did psychic work non-stop, co-produced punk rock storytelling shows and travelled out of town at least a couple of weekends a month for gigs at dance festivals.

I was so busy that he only time I ever saw my friends was if we were working together. My entire social life took place *backstage.* My sixtieth birthday party was at a gig, my witchy burlesque show "Belle, Book And Candle" which actually, was my favorite place to be once a month. The wildest birthday present I got was from Greg, but I hadn't even seen *him* in so long, that I found out about it on Instagram! In honor of my sixtieth, he'd gotten my name tattooed… *across his face.*

The only moments of quiet I ever had to myself were on long haul flights on the way to gigs… when I'd literally pass out in my seat. I was so sleep deprived those little naps felt like a two week vacation. Occasionally, I'd wake up and catch a glimpse of a half-finished movie. Usually it'd be an in-flight staple: a vapid, family friendly Rom-Com. These films were not my preferred genre at all, but sometimes, they'd make my mind drift to thinking about who my perfect make-believe love interest would be.

There were absolutely no options for me for me in entertainment or the occult, both were populated by gay men and straight women. I decided that whoever the new Romantic Interest was, they'd be all stable and *normal,* maybe even corporate, and I would be the creative, crazy person in the relationship. As the plane landed, I'd snap back to reality, realizing I didn't have any time for sleep, let alone dating, or even a fling.

Once again, the universe had a surprise in store for me. Through a string of synchronicities, much to my surprise, I somehow acquired a boyfriend, *a rock'n'roll boyfriend* no less. This was plot twist I hadn't anticipated like…at all. It was, in fact, the very *last* thing I wanted.

The first time I saw Lucifer, not his real name, obviously, was roughly twenty years ago at a Hollywood dive. He was so dangerously hot that I asked everyone within a twenty-foot radius, *Who the fuck is that?* The only thing that prevented me from swooping in on him was the blonde on his arm… and the way I behaved back in those days, that probably wouldn't have stopped me by the time I finished my drink. In hindsight, I'm shocked that it did.

Soon after, I saw him play for the first time. Not surprisingly, the front of the stage was packed with girls. Meanwhile, I hung out in back, just watching the spectacle unfold as the red flags I was seeing in 3D so fully covered the walls of the club, it was like an imaginary Christo installation.

Eventually, Lucifer and I were introduced by a mutual friend, but by that time, I had a serious boyfriend. I was also in the midst of exchanging my rock'n'roll debauchery in favor of the much healthier dancer's lifestyle. By the early 2000s I'd totally opted out of Music Biz shit, swapping touring with my own bands for travelling the world to teach and perform belly dance and burlesque. For fifteen years, I was gone for months a stretch; never in LA for more than a couple of days at a time.

Since dance touring wasn't like a band going out on the road, none of my gigs were sequential: I continent-hopped on a regular basis. I was so jet-lagged I could feel my IQ points drop alarmingly each time I took a trip. I had family and friends in LA that I literally hadn't seen in *years*. Even though I was still travelling a considerable amount in 2019, I made the decision counteract my All Work And No Play tendencies by vowing to go out to socialize once or twice a week.

One night as I was leaving an art opening, with one foot already in the ride share car I'd called, I spotted Lucifer on the sidewalk. I hadn't seen him in at least a decade and a half, but he still he looked hot as *hell*...pun very much intended. Asking the driver to wait, I hopped out to say hello and had a quick peck on the cheek before re-entering the car. During the ride home, it briefly flashed through my mind that maybe I should've cancelled the ride, but I quickly dismissed it as fantasy.

A few days later, after a long day of back-to-back Tarot and energy work sessions, I broke my habitual decompression routine. Instead of collapsing on the couch with my cats or taking a hike in the hills, I decided to take a walk. For some mysterious reason, I didn't change into my usual ratty leggings and sneakers. Instead, I found myself automatically brushing my hair and applying fresh lipstick. Grabbing my keys, I headed down the street at a swift clip.

It was a balmy late summer night and all the quaint sidewalk cafes in my 'hood were packed with hipsters. Then, from behind, I sensed eyes focusing on me just before hearing the words,

"Wow, twice in one week..."

Stopping dead in my tracks, I recognized Lucifer's voice before I even turned around. In a matter of minutes, he asked if I was single. We went and got popsicles; it felt comfy and we laughed a lot, hanging out on the street talking until well after dark. He asked if I lived nearby and offered to walk me home. I stopped at my street; he pointed out his place, leaving me with a little peck and squeeze. It turned out we lived so close to each other; it was nothing short of *ridiculous.*

The second I got inside my house, I spun into what could only be described as an existential crisis. With all the synchronicities I'd experienced in my life, this one threw me for a loop. Though I had no intention of backsliding into the lifestyle I'd given up so long ago, I was still immensely attracted to him. But I was a Different Person now and *way* too busy for that type of debauched rock'n'roll shenanigans.

Plus, I wasn't used to *regular* dating at all…I mean, not that we'd be *doing* that or anything. I'd only been on five dates in my entire life, and they were all disastrous. My only relationship experience came directly from punk rock. Whenever my all-girl band The Screaming Sirens went on tour, it was always the same. If any of us slept with guys from the bands we were touring with (and hello, that was *inevitable*) it was either the start of a relationship, or a one-night stand, which always made the rest of the tour pretty awkward. I was over and done with that crap for good.

Lucifer started texting to ask me out; I declined a few times, due to my obligations. Once I even wrote "Not Tonight Satan". I've always said yes to synchronicity, it's a green light from the universe, but I was gun shy and apprehensive about starting *anything* up with him. It took a bunch of dancers at a festival in Hawaii to convince me to give it a whirl, so I finally did. During our first *real* date, there was great conversation and even more synchronicities, and I started to let my guard down. By the time he grabbed me and pressed me up against a wall, kissing me in the middle of the street, any doubts I had completely vanished.

We started seeing each other regularly. Lucifer was fun, smart, and we both had a sarcastic sense of humor. Like the handsome devil he was, he led me into temptation. He was somewhat of a handful, but then, I was too; both of us were used to being the center of attention. Sometimes there was a power struggle with wisecracks and sexual undertones. When we went out, our energy was so wild, tongues would wag; people thought we were *crazy*.

If we'd been teenagers, our text threads would've gotten us grounded for life. And if we'd gotten together when we first met,

I was thoroughly convinced we'd both be dead.

A few months later, I was in the midst of teaching a Tarot class series to novices who, after the first few sessions, were already well on the way to becoming completely and utterly obsessed. Like most people who teach, I always used the Rider Waite Smith deck for instruction; they're the most famous Tarot cards in the world, it's the perfect starting point for beginners. Lavishly illustrated by artist Pamela Colman Smith, the deck features compelling scenes and characters ranging from beautiful, mystical women to devious-looking villains. Published in 1909, they've been reprinted countless times by many companies. Almost every modern Tarot deck is based upon Pamela Colman-Smith's ethereal art. Her work is loaded with so many visual cues that even a child could read the cards just by looking at them...which is precisely why the deck has been so popular for well over a hundred years.

My class had already been through the archetypes of the Major Arcana and the four suits of the Minor Arcana. In this particular session, we'd been exploring the rich symbology and it had taken up almost all of the two-hour session. I'd gone over crescent moons, castles, sphinxes, stars, water, blindfolds, deities, clouds... you name it and we'd explored it. Just as I was about to assign homework and wrap up the class, a woman in the back raised her hand, saying,

"I think you left something out because you haven't talked about one of the symbols yet...it's like a curlicue or some kind of squiggle."

My mind immediately went to Celtic symbols such as spirals, *triskelions,* and *triquetas*, but the Rider Waite Smith cards didn't contain any of them. Stumped, I asked her if she was working with

a more modern deck.

"It's the same cards you're using", she insisted,

"And this symbol is on each one of them!"

Without a clue what she was referring to, I asked her to bring the deck up to show me. At my desk, she fanned the cards, pointing out the Mystery Symbol. The "squiggle" she was referring to turned out to be Pamela Colman Smith's signature, which indeed is on every card. Curiosity piqued, the rest of the class surged forward to get a look, but the woman who'd asked the question still looked a little dubious. I picked up the *Smith-Waite Centennial* deck, which has an enlarged version of the signature printed on the backs of the cards. Holding it up for the students, I examined it too; it was elegant, and it did look like a stylized sigil.

"You know, this'd actually make a great tattoo!", I commented.

A different student came forward, asking if she could get a closer look. As she reached for the card, I noticed the intricate, gorgeously executed Arabic *Hamsa* tattooed on her arm.

"Well, while we're on the subject of tattoos," I mused,

"I can't *believe* I've been a belly dancer for over thirty years and have always wanted a *Hamsa* tattoo but never gotten one, now I'm having major Tattoo Shame!"

A second later, my phone got an alert. Since Lucifer liked sending lewd memes when he knew I was teaching, I just took a cursory glance. The text wasn't from him, but what I saw made me gasp.

It was from my tattoo artist Baba Austin, saying he'd be out of town for two months, so if I felt like getting any ink done, I should come in right away. Though we'd known each other for years, it wasn't like Baba texted me that often and he never needed to solicit tattoos, his client base was huge. The timing was uncanny. My face registered such shock, that a few students asked if everything was ok. As soon as I read the text out loud, the entire room turned cacophonous with everyone talking at once.

"I'm gonna call him right now and book an appointment to get Pamela Colman-Smith's signature and a *Hamsa*," I declared, to applause and cheers from the whole class.

Baba picked up on the first ring; he was on speaker phone as I told him the story.

"Shut the fuck up!" he said, with all the students listening.

"I know you don't believe me," I continued,

"But I've got over twenty witnesses here, and they'll vouch for me… right, you guys?"

The entire class screamed "Yes!" in unison.

Later that day, Lucifer texted to ask what I was doing the next night. When I mentioned I had an appointment for some new ink, he joked that I should get his name tattooed on my face. I answered back, kidding that it was obvious he was simply seething with jealousy over someone loving me enough to get my name across their cheeks…. because *he* couldn't claim that, now could he? He answered with a photo of a vintage motel sign that had CS on it, suggesting that his initials would make a great tattoo no matter *where* I got it. My answer, of course, was LOL.

Vintage Tattoo Art Parlor is an enclave of Old School Cool as well as one of one of the more established businesses in the rapidly becoming gentrified Highland Park area of Los Angeles. The place looks like an art director or cinematographer's vision of the perfect, classic tattoo shop. The walls are covered in traditional flash and yellowing old Polaroids, while the bathroom walls are scrawled with graffiti from satisfied clients. Sketch pads, art books and a plethora of tattoo magazines are piled high on the well-worn wooden counters. An oversized ceiling fan whirs overhead; '70s and '80s LA punk rock is always blasting.

The shop is usually bustling with prospective customers, but oddly, that night I was the only client there. Baba and I joked around as he sized the *Hamsa* to fit my arm. A woman strolled in without an appointment; Bob, the other tattoo artist on duty, asked what she had in mind. When she said she said she wanted a *Hamsa*, Baba, Bob and I looked at each other incredulously. As the woman's ink got started in the other room, Baba talked over the loud buzz of his co-worker's tattoo machine,

"That's so crazy! Nobody's asked for a *Hamsa* in years, now, we've got two in one night!"

I thought: *Thass jest how I roll!*

Taking a break between tattoos, I ran out for pizza while Baba sized Pamela Colman-Smith's signature for me. By the time I got back, it was ready to go. He held the stencil he'd made up to my right wrist, near the Ouija Board planchette he'd done a few months earlier. It fit perfectly, so he applied it to my skin. Because the location was on the outside of my arm, the most comfortable position for me to be in was face down, with my wrist propped up on a little pillow. As he swapped out the needles in his machine and started it up, he was curious about the meaning of the design. I explained it was the signature of the woman who'd created the world's most famous Tarot deck.

"Oh," he replied, "I thought it was some sort of witchy thing, like

 a magic sigil."

I felt the burn of the fine needles piercing my skin, tracing the stylized signature. Baba's work was always precise and fast. Even though I was face down and couldn't see it, I knew from sensing the needle following the curves and the twists of the design that my tattoo was almost finished.

"There!" Baba said, "Sit up and have a look."

Yet again, the universe had a surprise in store for me. As I admired my new tattoo in the mirror, he inquired,

"So, the artist's initials are P-C-S?"

It wasn't until that very moment that I realized that I now had my first initial and both of Lucifer's marked into my skin indelibly.

THE FOOL.

THE FOOL

The wildest Tarot reading I've ever done took place at a magician's club smack dab in the middle of the Hollywood Boulevard Walk Of Fame. Located in a historic building that'd once housed silent film starlets, Black Rabbit Rose was a hipster version of the legendary Magic Castle, and also employed several of their world class performers. But since it didn't require membership like the Castle, along with magic aficionados who frequented it, the joint was a magnet for vapid Instagram influencers, sunburned tourists staying in the Air B&B rooms upstairs and a non-stop parade of Boulevard Trash. On any given night, there were aging, also-ran local rockers, wannabe hip hop stars in knock-off designer sweats reeking of weed, small time street drug dealers and the crackheads who trailed them like bloodhounds.

The space was intimate, dimly lit by dripping candles in wrought iron wall sconces. The lobby décor included antique magician's accoutrements, vintage Houdini posters and the classic arcade attraction, the robotic fortuneteller Zoltar, located directly across from my Tarot table. There's an undeniably spooky feeling in that part of Hollywood and in that building in particular; it actually was part of the reason I took the job as House Fortuneteller. The moment I walked in for the first time, I knew without a doubt the place was extremely haunted. Every so often, before the place opened for the evening, or around closing time, the Zoltar machine would unexpectedly come to life *by itself* scaring the shit out of me as it blasted its trademark recording: "Let Me See Into Your Future!"

While Zoltar attracted groups of drunks spilling cocktails while taking sloppy selfies, I always had a crowd of well-behaved and curious observers clustered around my table watching me work.

One night, an attractive couple lingered a long time, through a number of my clients, looking on in fascination as I laid the cards out and interpreted them. They stood out to me in the crowd: both were tall and slender, very good looking. I saw a golden glow radiating around them like a divine nimbus in a medieval fresco. The woman was a doe-eyed honey blonde in floaty summer dress; the man could've been a dashing, handsome pirate if he'd been dressed differently. When I had a lull, they stepped forward almost hesitantly, inquiring if I could do a reading for two people at the same time.

"Sure," I replied, "I do couples readings all the time."

Exchanging a quick nervous glance, they said simultaneously,

"We're not a couple!"

I assured them that couple or not, I'd do a tandem reading if that's what they wanted, so the guy grabbed a chair from a nearby table, laid a few neatly folded bills on the table and they sat down. As I shuffled, I instructed them to say their names aloud and tell me their birthdays.

The cards pulled no punches, delivering a message so clear and direct that even a novice could've read it in seconds. Two Of Cups: relationships, attraction, harmony, compatibility; The Lovers: love, romance, deep connection, mind-blowing sex; Eight Of Wands: infatuation, obsession, the sensation being swept off your feet. The next cards were matched pairs, which I always consider to be an indication of soulmates: I pulled The Empress and The Emperor, who are a couple in the Major Arcana, followed by The King and Queen of Cups, the highest masculine and feminine energy of Cups, the Minor Arcana suit that correlates to the element of water, representing emotions, feelings, love and intuition. Then I pulled The Star-hope, faith, magic and blessings, and the Wheel Of Fortune which represents fate, destiny, synchronicity, luck and good fortune. The outcome was Ace of Cups; joy, happiness; engagements, weddings, conception, baby showers and celebrations.

Normally, I take a little time to look at the spread, noting how each card interconnects with those around it before voicing my interpretation. In this case, I didn't *need* to; the cards were loud and clear; in fact, they were *way* over the top, practically hollering at me. Without even thinking about what I was going to say, I surprised myself by blurting out,

"Are you guys *sure* you're not a couple? Are you testing me?"

Taken aback, they both shifted uncomfortably in their chairs, exchanging another skittish glance before staring at me, each with eyes as wide as anime characters.

Valiantly attempting damage control, I excused myself, explaining that I usually didn't operate that way, blurting out a question. I paused for a drink of water before telling them the story the spread revealed. They followed along from card to card, eyes occasionally darting around the room uncomfortably or sneaking surreptitious glances at each other. By the end of the reading, they were nodding along with what I said, but still looked a bit nonplussed. Standing up in unison, they thanked me politely,

before vanishing into the bar.

Moments later, they were back.

"Please humor me," the man said, tossing a crisp new twenty onto my table,

"Will you shuffle the cards and just pick one? I know it sounds weird, but I really need you to do it!"

Tucking the bill into my bag, I got out a different deck, shuffling extensively before cutting it and pulling a card. With a graceful little flourish, I placed The Fool on the table. The man's eyes almost popped out of his head, right before he emitted such a loud, extended *unearthly* howl that made the entire population of the crowded lobby whirl around in unison to see what the fuck was going down.

"Nooooooo!" he bellowed in disbelief, like someone who'd just lost thousands of dollars at a roulette table.

Grabbing his head with both hands, shaking it vigorously he shrieked,

"I can't *believe* it... how can this even be possible?"

Turning quickly on his heels, he plowed through the crowd blindly as he ran back into the bar.

The woman sank back into the chair she'd vacated moments before, a dazed look on her face. Both of us watched in silence as a waitress toting a load of bar towels and a busboy armed with a mop and bucket invaded the to clean up the carnage like a triage team at the scene of a major disaster. They scurried around changing soaked tablecloths, sweeping up the broken glass from the multitude of drinks spilled when nearby customers panicked, attempting to escape from what appeared to be the beginning of a bar fight. Everyone remaining in the immediate area heaved a collective sigh of relief and business returned to usual. One of the club's roving magicians popped by my table to perform a card trick; the woman politely shook her head and waved him away.

Her eyes meeting mine, she inquired,

"Would you like to know what all that was about?"

The backstory she provided turned out to be even more incredible than everything that'd just taken place. She told me in hushed tones that they'd met quite recently on a dating app, taking their conversation offline and into texts and calls quickly. After a few rounds of flirtatious conversations, they decided to get together in person. Their first date went so well, they immediately made a second one to go to the historic Farmer's Market in LA's Fairfax district. She explained that the First Date had taken place earlier today and that their evening out tonight was a spur of the moment continuation of this afternoon.

After spending time browsing around the kitschy souvenir stalls, the couple entered a shop; the first thing they saw as they walked in was a wine display placed directly in front of the store's entrance. Each of the bottles were labelled with a Major Arcana Tarot card.

With an earnest look, she told me that a couple of months earlier, she'd been introduced to Tarot by a friend who'd gifted her a deck. She'd gotten into it quickly, becoming obsessed. She'd spent a lot of time studying books, doing daily card pulls for herself, kept a journal and couldn't stop herself from cruising through Tarot sites on the internet. When she saw the wine, she'd gotten really excited. Her paramour noticed and told her he'd buy a bottle for her. She'd selected The Fool, informing him she'd picked it out because it represented a new beginning.

Together, they decided to nix lunch at The Farmer's Market in favor of making it at her place and drinking the wine, so they bought a bunch of produce at the farm stands and headed home. On the way, he playfully ribbed her about the cards, telling her he didn't believe in "all that woo stuff". At her apartment, they chopped the veggies together, talking and laughing the whole time. As she tossed and dressed the salad, he set the table and opened the wine, asking her for a pen before telling her to get out her Tarot cards.

"But wait!", she called from her bedroom,

"I thought you said didn't believe in them?"

"I'm doing an experiment!" he answered.

She placed the deck on the table as he poured the wine, they toasted, feasted and got a little tipsy. After they finished, he cleared the table, poured them each another glass and commanded her to shuffle the cards until he asked her to stop. Finally, he told her to cut the deck, pick a card and place it on the table face down. They both stared at it for a little while until she asked if she could turn it over; he nodded.

It was The Fool.

The man did a double take. His eyebrows shot up as his jaw dropped; he got up slowly and deliberately, pulling a folded slip of paper from his pocket, setting it on the table next to The Fool, demanding her to read it out loud.

The note said:

If the card you picked is The Fool, we are meant to be together forever.

"So," the woman said sincerely, looking me directly in the eyes while fidgeting nervously with her hair,

"That's why he just did that. I'm really sorry it caused such a commotion, but I just *had* to tell you. Thank you for the reading and the extra card, it confirmed everything that happened today. I guess…I'm going to go back in there with him."

Immediately, I got the impression that they'd spent the rest of the afternoon in bed, hence the golden glow I'd noticed around them, but I left it unsaid. Instead, I thanked her for the amazing story and wished her good luck. She squeezed my hand and went into the bar.

The magic show had started in the theater, so the lobby was empty except for Zoltar and me. I packed up my cards, candles and sign and folded my sparkly tablecloth. As I zipped up my gig bag, I was startled to see the man standing at the doorway to the bar with a huge grin on his face.

"We'd like to have a drink with you," he said, courteously,

"Will you please join us?"

In years of reading cards at parties, corporate events, and clubs, I've never once had a drink with any of my clients, but this time I made an exception. I followed him into the bar and slid into the cozy booth where the woman was waiting with a big smile on her face. An ice bucket holding an expensive bottle of champagne sat on the tabletop flanked with three coupe glasses. As he poured the bubbly, the couple exchanged a happy glance.

We raised our glasses in a toast to The Fool, and barely containing their excitement, they announced that they'd just gotten engaged.

FINIS

ACKNOWLEDGEMENTS

Love, gratitude and magick to the following people:

To my lifelong bestie, keeper of secrets and publisher, Iris Berry-"It *is* babe, isn't it? To my sister, Eddie Gehman Kohan, my "son" Morgan Hudson; my darling Devilla, the LLL Coven: Kelly Morse, Natasha Vetlugin, Kristina Nekyia, and Vanessa Burgundy. True Lovies Bill Mullen and Todd Noaker; to my kitty baby daddy James Packard. To Margaret Cho; Gregory "BKB" Barnett, Jeffoto and Jason Thompson. To my sister from another mister and Divination Nation partner Crystal Ravenwolf. To Theresa Kereakes, The Go-Go's especially Belinda Carlisle and Jane Wiedlin; Brad Dunning, Kid Congo Powers, Anna Statman and Joan Stern: thank you all for *decades* of love, adventures and non-stop laughter. To Steve Balderson, Paul Jordan, Iva Said, Adriana Leal, Larry Johnson, Daniel Marti, Baba Austin, my birthday twin Gus Jafolla and Carlos Adley. To Pamela Des Barres for constant inspiration. To my Belle, Book & Candle co-producer and bestie Shana Leilani for the Showgirl Stage Sorcery we created and our coven of amazing dancers. To Indian Hill Cemetery, my childhood refuge. To Hollywood Forever Cemetery, my adult refuge and all the animals and spirits residing there. To my exalted Ramones Duck partner Coyote Shivers for keeping me sane-*I use the term loosely*-during the pandemic. To Carrie Bible, Micheline Cherie, Daniel Feld, Stella Bridge, and Stefano, Sherri and Scott. To my Summer of Lockdown buddies Victor, Sarah, Lee, Colin and Nat. To the great folks at Pantheon Podcasts and to the marvelous people at El Cid. To Joshua at Rock Roll Repeat for making the fab shirts, to John Doe, Tom Desavia, Peter Bebergal, Divine Hand Jim aka James Barker, Maverick Cadaverick and my ventriloquism soulmate Dana Gould. To all the lovely witches at The Green Man Store. To all my supernatural sisters: Pinky "Merve" DeVille, Kira Von Sutra, Liz Rhodes, Kellie Sue Peters,

Marcella Kroll, Kristen J. Sollee, Madame Pamita, "Gold Dust" Emily Rick, Theresa "The Tarot Lady" Reed, Lisa Derrick, Vicky Adams, Rebecca Fenn, Lina Lecaro, Kimberly Kim, Gaby Herstik, Malice Stardust, Diamond Debbie, Meline, Ursula Undress, Kari Krome, Augusta Avallone and Dusty Paik...*would*, my Pango. To Surreyya Hada, Valarie Bermudez, Angie Alaska, Diamondback Annie, Lux La Croix, Lulu Bombshell, Coco Ono and Danielle G., Sherry Wheatley, Alli Ruth, Erin Alden- and all my Pantheon peeps. To Armen Ra, my princess; to Karie Bible and our sleek boyfriend, Closeup The Cemetery Cat. To d my synchronicity-sister Wendi L. Eckert, Annie aka Sharmuta Please and to wonderful Lisa Derrick. To my feline children: Ghost, Carmen, Magick Lovey Puss aka The Fuzz...and to their brother Beeper, who crossed the Rainbow Bridge far too soon-but who a slept in a basket every night next to me as I wrote these stories; rest in pounce and power, my Big Tabby Boy.

Every one of you supported me during the writing of this book more than you'll ever know.

MORE ABOUT ROCK 'N' ROLL WITCH

Whether she is frantically recalling Siouxsie & The Banshees lyrics in order to get the words to the Lord's Prayer right to chase away a bedroom-invading poltergeist or discovering that under the façade of a haunted amusement park lies a *real* haunted amusement park, Pleasant Gehman, in *Rock 'N' Roll Witch*, takes us on an often thrilling, often hilarious, always entertaining journey through her supernaturally-soaked existence.

And therein lies the catch. In these pages, Pleasant performs a jujitsu flip on the old expression, "seeing is believing." As the book clearly illustrates, it's not that she sees what she believes… It's that she believes. So she sees. And you will too!

-Dana Gould

Emmy Award winning writer, *The Simpsons*

Pleasant Gehman could write the phonebook and I'd read it. Her little black book would ooze with sensational names and numbers that would make a grown man blush-mainly because there would be a wild story connected to each name. In *Rock & Roll Witch*, she ties together tales of cemetery adventures from childhood through her wild days as a Hollywood punk rocker in the 1970s and beyond. Her language is thrilling, and the stories remind me of great pulp fiction, except it's all real!

- John Doe, Austin, TX

Move over, Edgar Allan, there's a new bitch in town.

Pleasant has been my dear friend for over forty years, and I kid you not when I say she has had more weird things happen to her than all my other friends combined. Of course, her love of scary and weird adventures, lively imagination, and attraction to strange people, places and things account for some of that... but not all. She has some kind of electric current in her body that routinely stops watches and small appliances. She is faithfully followed by the number 1111, to the point that goes way past coincidence. She routinely finds herself in psychedelic situations, with or without the help of pharmaceuticals.

She is a national treasure to weirdos. She deserves every accolade bestowed on her and all the rabid adoration her fans lavish on her. I too adore her and her story telling and if you are holding this book, I know that you will too.

-Jane Wiedlin

"Pleasant Gehman has lived the spookiest, witchiest, most riotous punk rock life of any woman I know. In her book, *Rock & Roll Witch*, she shares her craziest and creepiest tales yet! One minute, the hair is standing up on the back of your neck, while the next you're laughing so hard you're doubling over on the floor. Pleasant is a captivating storyteller with an ability to deliver the goods with such detail that you feel you're along for the wild ride."

-Theresa Reed, author of *Tarot: No Questions Asked - Mastering the Art of Intuitive Reading*

Pleasant is a master storyteller of the true tales of her life as a muse and maker in Los Angeles. In *Rock' N' Roll Witch*, she brings us a cauldron filled to the brim with her real-life supernatural encounters that will make you shiver, induce knowing laughs, and may even bring a tear to your eye. Reading this book is like sidling up to the bar in a dark and dangerous dive, sitting next to a stranger who begins telling you a story that draws you in and weaves a magnetic web of fascination. You'll find yourself utterly captivated, waiting to hear what will happen next. This book proves that ghost stories are not just "stories." It's a true mystical, magical page-turner that will leave you spellbound.

- Madame Pamita, author of *The Book of Candle Magic* (Llewellyn) and *Madame Pamita's Magical Tarot* (Weiser)

I've always known Pleasant to be a bit of a witch! We used to frequent the witchcraft stores to buy things to put inside our mojo bags, books and items to cast spells on boys. Years later she reinvented herself as a belly dancer/ghostbuster, which is an awesome combination-she impressed me as her psychic skills improved ten-fold. I lived in a notoriously haunted building in West Hollywood. I'll never forget that moment in my bedroom, she was holding a device that was sort of like a transistor radio, trying to focus on a frequency to communicate with whatever was going on, when this voice came out of it saying, "Help me". Just thinking about it gives me shivers…I'm thrilled she's sharing a lifetime of stories of paranormal experiences, she's a great storyteller.

- Belinda Carlisle

ABOUT PLEASANT GEHMAN

Pleasant Gehman is a true renaissance woman. A lifelong multi-disciplinary artist, she is a writer, professional dancer, actor, psychic, musician, and painter.

A Hollywood rock 'n' roll icon, during the 1970s, she was one of the first punks in Los Angeles, documenting the scene she helped create in her fanzine *Lobotomy*, which lead to writing for the top mainstream rock publications. During the 1980s and early '90s she toured fronting her three bands, all of whom released multiple recordings: The Screaming Sirens, The Ringling Sisters and Honk If Yer Horny. Concurrently, she was the talent booker for the seminal Los Angeles punk/alternative clubs Cathay De Grande and Raji's, as well as producing large scale shows at other venues.

Since the early 1990s, using the stage name Princess Farhana, she has appeared internationally as a professional belly dance and burlesque performer and instructor touring in China, Australia, Turkey, several times in Egypt, and constantly across Europe, The United Kingdom and North America. She's danced and acted in numerous motion pictures, appeared in music videos and on television shows and has been featured in many documentaries on belly dance and burlesque, performing and as an interview subject. In 2009, she was the sole focus of director Steve Balderson's feature length documentary *Underbelly: A Year In The Life Of Princess Farhana,* released worldwide in theaters as well as on DVD.

A practicing witch, her work as a psychic, Tarot reader and energy healer has been life-long; she currently shares her gifts with clients worldwide.

From the age of sixteen onwards, Pleasant has been a journalist, cultural commentator and historian, with hundreds of articles published nationally and internationally on everything from rock 'n' roll, art, fashion and pop culture to the paranormal. She covered the OJ Simpson trial, and has done immersion journalism, spending weeks to months covering homeless teenagers, circuses, drag performers, stunt people, magicians, and porn stars... to name a few. Her memoirs, short stories and poetry have been widely anthologized in literary journals and CDs, including on her solo spoken word CD *Ruined.*

In May 2017, Pleasant and co-producer Shana Leilani created *Belle, Book and Candle*, the first and only burlesque show run by and for witches. It became a hub for the Los Angeles pagan community and continued with virtual shows during 2020. The show continues to sell out monthly. In March 2020, Pleasant launched her popular podcast *The Devil's Music*, which explores the intersection of rock'n'roll and the occult. It is available across all podcasting platforms.

Pleasant is the author and/or editor of eight books, including The Los Angeles Times Best Seller *The Underground Guide To Los Angeles*, *The Belly Dance Handbook* and the memoir *Showgirl Confidential: My Life Onstage, Backstage And On The Road* (Sept. 2013, Punk Hostage Press)

She authored her own chapters in John Doe and Tom Desavia's *Under The Big Black Sun: A Personal History Of LA Punk* and *More Fun In The New World: The Unmaking And Legacy Of LA Punk.* She appears in photos and as an interview subject in several other books on punk rock as well, both published and forthcoming.

Pleasant lives in Hollywood, California with her spoiled rescue cats.

www.pleasantgehman.com
www.princessfarhana.com
Instagram:@princessofhollywood
@belle_book_and_candle
@ramonesducks
Twitter:@PleasantGehman1
Facebook: @PleasantGehman

Photo by: Christina L. Hughes

MORE BOOKS ON PUNK HOSTAGE PRESS

Danny Baker
> *Fractured* - 2012

A Razor
> *Better Than a Gun in A Knife* Fight - 2012
> *Drawn Blood: Collected Works*
> *From D.B.P.LTD., 1985-1995* - 2012
> *Beaten Up Beaten Down* - 2012
> *Small Catastrophes in A Big World* - 2012
> *Half- Century Status* - 2013
> *Days of Xmas Poems* - 2014
> *Puro Purismo* - 2021

Iris Berry
> *The Daughters of Bastards* - 2012
> *All That Shines Under the Hollywood Sign* – 2019
> *The Trouble with Palm Trees* – 2021
> *Gas Station Etiquette* - 2022

C.V. Auchterlonie
> *Impress* - 2012

Yvonne De la Vega
> *Tomorrow, Yvonne - Poetry & Prose for Suicidal Egoists* - 2012

Carolyn Srygley- Moore
> *Miracles Of the Blog: A Series* - 2012

Rich Ferguson
> 8th & Agony -2012

Jack Grisham
> *Untamed* -2013
> *Code Blue: A Love Story* ~ 2014
> *Pulse of the World. Arthur Chance, Punk Rock Detective* - 2021

Dennis Cruz
> *Moth Wing Tea* - 2013
> *The Beast Is We* - 2018

Frank Reardon
> *Blood Music* - 2013

Pleasant Gehman
> *Showgirl Confidential* – 2013

Hollie Hardy
> *How To Take a Bullet and Other Survival Poems* – 2014

Joel Landmine
> *Yeah, Well...* – 2014
> *Things Change* – 2021

MORE BOOKS ON PUNK HOSTAGE PRESS

A.D. Winans
>*Dead Lions* – 2014

Michele McDannold
>*Stealing The Midnight from A Handful of Days* – 2014

S.A. Griffin
>*Dreams Gone Mad with Hope* - 2014

SB Stokes
>*History Of Broken Love Things* – 2014

Nadia Bruce- Rawlings
>*Scars* - 2014
>*Driving in The Rain* - 2020

Lee Quarnstrom
>*WHEN I WAS A DYNAMITER, Or, how a Nice Catholic Boy Became a Merry Prankster, a Pornographer, and a Bridegroom Seven Times* - 2014

Alexandra Naughton
>*I Will Always Be Your Whore/Love Songs for Billy Corgan* - 2014
>*You Could Never Objectify Me More Than I've Already Objectified Myself* -2015

Maisha Z Johnson
>*No Parachutes to Carry Me Home* - 2015

Michael Marcus
>*#1 Son and Other Stories* - 2017

Danny Garcia
>*LOOKING FOR JOHNNY, The Legend of Johnny Thunders* - 2018

William S. Hayes
>*Burden of Concrete* - 2020
>*King of the Road* - 2021

Todd Moore
>*Dillinger's Thompson* - 2020

Dan Denton
>*$100-A-Week Motel* - 2021

Jack Henry
>Driving W/ Crazy, living with madness – 2021
>*My Life with The Dwarves, How I Drank, Fought & Fucked My Way Around the World* - 2021

Joe Donnelly
>*So Cal. Dispatches from the End of The World* - 2022

Patrick O'Neil
>*Anarchy at The Circle K – On the Road With* Dead Kennedys, T.S.O.L., Flipper, Subhumans… and Heroin – 2022